Take Action

Thought Triggers to Improve Your Business Life

(Simple Tricks Validated by Science to Defeat Procrastination While Having Fun)

Courtney Freeman

Published By **Darby Connor**

Courtney Freeman

All Rights Reserved

Take Action: Thought Triggers to Improve Your Business Life (Simple Tricks Validated by Science to Defeat Procrastination While Having Fun)

ISBN 978-1-7774561-7-7

No part of this guidebook shall be reproduced in any form without permission in writing from the publisher except in the case of brief quotations embodied in critical articles or reviews.

Legal & Disclaimer

The information contained in this book is not designed to replace or take the place of any form of medicine or professional medical advice. The information in this book has been provided for educational & entertainment purposes only.

The information contained in this book has been compiled from sources deemed reliable, and it is accurate to the best of the Author's knowledge; however, the Author cannot guarantee its accuracy and validity and cannot be held liable for any errors or omissions. Changes are periodically made to this book. You must consult your doctor or get professional medical advice before using any of the suggested remedies, techniques, or information in this book.

Upon using the information contained in this book, you agree to hold harmless the Author from and against any damages, costs, and expenses, including any legal fees potentially resulting from the application of any of the information provided by this guide. This disclaimer applies to any damages or injury caused by the use and application, whether directly or indirectly, of any advice or information presented, whether for breach of contract, tort, negligence, personal injury, criminal intent, or under any other cause of action.

You agree to accept all risks of using the information presented inside this book. You need to consult a professional medical practitioner in order to ensure you are both able and healthy enough to participate in this program.

Table Of Contents

Chapter 1: Some Words About Procrastination O Procrastination In Our Environment 1

Chapter 2: Procrastination In Our Daily Life 27

Chapter 3: Mistakes To Avoid At All Costs 42

Chapter 4: Action-Oriented Self-Talk 69

Chapter 5: Transforming Goals Into Habits 77

Chapter 6: Make A Plan Take Action Now And Get Things Done 86

Chapter 7: Get Action Right Now Using Mind Maps... 90

Chapter 8: Use Vision Boards 95

Chapter 9: It Is Fun To Act At The Right Time And Place 100

Chapter 10: Now And Control Your Life 105

Chapter 11: Now Look At Time And Place 110

Chapter 12: Suck It Up And Move Stop Refusing 115

Chapter 13: Get A New Attitude For Real 121

Chapter 14: You Have The Ability 125

Chapter 15: Getting Out Of The Loop ... 131

Chapter 16: Selling A Service 169

Chapter 1: Some Words About Procrastination O Procrastination In Our Environment

In Western societies, people typically establish short, medium and long-term objectives related to their healthcare, work, education as well. It is a matter of creating a strategy to reach them, which could be explicitly or implicitly along with an estimate of the time necessary to accomplish the goal. If these plans can be completed within the stipulated time and with a positive outcome, the benefits from these actions are likely to become evident.

In contrast, negative effects are heightened if the planned and future-oriented actions cannot be implemented in the anticipated time.

The majority of people "leave the future to do the things they are able to do today" can be viewed as irresponsible or lazy appreciated by other people who have the same attitude. Lack of focus for completing tasks planned in the expected time is correlated with a certain uncomfortable feelings. If this happens throughout the vital areas of life the person is likely to delay.

Procrastination is a common habit of putting off the beginning and end of the tasks that were scheduled to be completed within an agreed upon time. Procrastination tends to be associated with feelings of discomfort. It is an issue of lack of responsibility as well as time control and can be an issue of self-regulation in the affective, cognitive, and behavior levels.

This is widespread in the university academic world, as a lot of academic functions have to be conducted within a specified time period.

The student who isn't able to finish homework at the correct time will be able to complete other obligations, such as buying tickets for a show or remaining at the set time with his friends. The habit of putting off schoolwork is often referred to as academic procrastination. This is widely recognized in the field of education but not much discussed by universities' direction departments.

Professionally Companies that fail to take their time are at risk of reducing the standard of their product or products or. The people who exhibit greater levels of procrastination are more likely to lose jobs quicker. It may also be related to the possibility of redundancies due to low contributions to performance or as the first employees who are dismissed as a result of cutbacks.

In the business world, each idea, project or document will come with deadlines for delivery and a promise of high-quality. Making these decisions late is not going to help the end results be top-quality.

While we might think delay can have a positive impact on our health, the truth is it's not.

A few of the adverse effects that procrastination may have on our mental and physical well-being are as follows, According to a psychologist Amat:

Having difficulty making choices.

Inability to resolve the issue.

A difficulty in dealing with stress in general.

Organizing is difficult.

Troubles trying to communicate one's personal needs.

It could lead to excessive levels of anxiety and anxiety.

Research has found it can increase the chance of developing cardiovascular diseases as well as high blood pressure.

The research conducted over the last 25 years has revealed that procrastination has become a prevalent problem within Western society, and is the general pattern. Everyone delays the beginning and end of tasks however, not everyone can be considered to be procrastinators.

People who procrastinate are all affected in a different or less amount. It is a sign that you know that the work must be accomplished, however motivation to complete it isn't produced within the planned time duration.

If it is a persistent habit, it can become an unhealthy living style. The estimates suggest that 15% of all adult males as well as women (meaning people who are part of studies that involve an ununiversitybased population of more than 18 years of age) are considered to be chronically procrastinators.

People engage in unnecessarily delayed completion of assignments in different contexts and settings. Two studies across cultures have revealed that within Australia, Peru, Spain as well as Spain, the United Kingdom, the United States as well as Venezuela the rate of chronic procrastination among adults ranges from 10.9 percentage to 16.1 percent.

O I PROCRASTINATE. YOU PROCRASTINATE, BUT WHAT IS IT?

The word "procrastination" originates from Latin procrastinate. It translates as "to put off until the next day" and is identified as the need to put off the commencement and conclusion of work that has to be completed within a specific duration of time for someone who is suffering from an unresolved uncomfortableness.

As definitions of procrastination stress the anxiety of delay in behavior and anxiety, the two elements of the definition must be viewed in conjunction. According to this perspective Procrastination is defined as an unintentional desire to put off tasks that must be completed. It is also delays that are not necessary for tasks which should be accomplished, particularly in cases where it's extended enough to cause feelings of discomfort.

Procrastination can be derived from behavior signs (e.g. absence of punctuality in appointment times or delays in the submission of academic documents) and, on the cognitive level, it is based on intentions to do tasks. It also involves "voluntarily delay in a plan of action in spite of the negative consequences this can bring about."

Procrastination is a term that refers to four distinct subdimensions: the affective response for pressure to act and cognitive procrastination decision and the ability of the individual to adhere to deadlines, and the ability to attain acceptable result. These subdimensions must be confirmed both psychometrically as well as theoretically.

Procrastination is defined as two main elements: mental stress that comes from the delay and time frame. In this way, we've studied the connection between procrastination and two kinds of temporal variables: time perspective as well as the time-based typology of the circadian.

As a rule, those who are procrastinators aren't focused on the future, and are primarily focused on the current. However at night, they tend to delay the tasks they need to complete until their most productive moment of the night, when they are in a social setting. It's fascinating to observe how the different time-related variables can be linked to procrastination. Procrastination due to indecision may be related to inability to maintain a balanced mental focus on the past, present as well as the future. Behavioral procrastination may be linked to a preferences for late night.

If you are a procrastinator, a time is logical and justified. However in the outside view this is not rational and may harm the image of the individual.

Procrastination occurs because of the gap between intent and action: it is something that the individual would prefer not to do, and this creates discomfort and has a negative impact on the way they live their lives. It is not a good idea to define "active procrastination" just a simple delay in things that are not causing uncomfortableness for the individual. The term "postponing" is used in conjunction with delay, or postponing for this type of activity.

There's a distinct difference between putting off a task as we all frequently perform, and the inclination to regularly delay the commencement or completion of work. If someone delays an action to get more details or delay an action because they have perform something essential prior to the deadline. If that is the case, those tactics are not that are procrastination-related. The delay or deferral of well-planned activities to accommodate different activities is not "active procrastination." In essence, it is a notion that incorporates two key elements throughout its definitions: delay in time as well as personal discomfort.

Occasionally, the procrastinator creates an array of mental beliefs that lead to excuses, overvaluations as well as self-sabotage behaviors to avoid performing the act.

Individuals who identify as slow-moving people often seek to curb the amount of time they spend on tasks by establishing realistic objectives and deadlines to finish projects within a sensible time duration. Yet it is true that the time necessary to finish the tasks are often overestimated.

Additionally, numerous research studies suggest the connection between procrastination and different personality traits, such as poor self-esteem, self-confidence and the tendency to be depressed or social anxiety. It can also lead to disordered impulsivity, stiffness in the behavior as well as a lack of motivation.

Procrastination is linked to two personality traits that are most prominent, excessive neuroticism and lack of responsibility and self-discipline, particularly low.

The tradition's origins

Procrastination is an issue in self-regulation and time arrangement. Whoever delays or rethinks making a choice is an evasive act.

The attitude of all or nothing

"There is only one winner and two losers. "

"There is just one correct approach."

"Do the right thing Or don't bother even once."

These statements are an attitude that promotes unproductive behaviour. Research about human behavior shows that the world isn't one of two colors, winning either way, bad or bad. In the majority of cases the way we live our lives is in the gray zone, which is somewhere between extremes.

The common but unfounded "All or nothing" attitude is the reason why billions of dollars are being paid in the world's casinos. Every bettor who plays all-or-nothing ends in a void.

This extreme mindset creates a number of the unconscious fears which we discussed earlier. The all-or-nothing mentality stalls the efforts of getting ourselves to a disciplined self as we fear the possibility of slipping (err).

Because the All or Nothing thought compares the fall to a stumble so we think this is more secure than not attempt to achieve the goals we set.

Furthermore, this system of belief in the success of a person means living a monotonous lifestyle of working addiction. Are you really interested in this? What about the aspect of self-control which tells you it is necessary to break down your big tasks into smaller pieces of tasks so you don't feel overwhelmed at first? Unfortunately, if all you're able to see is the whole of the massive undertaking, you'll be unable to start because you will not be able to sense the ease of each step you're taking; you have to take all this. The whole thing is a no-brainer that you tell you.

Because it's not possible to accomplish a project at once it's best to not even start any thing. Naturally. When you've got images hung "all or absolutely nothing" above your heads, there are motives to avoid the effort to achieve the gradual discipline demands.

Then, you subconsciously tell yourself that you'll end up being nothing or a loss if the plan you've devised doesn't succeed. If you think of yourself as a champion or fool, then everything will be defined as a matter of life and the end of life.

The tension created by this assertion alone will make you rethink your discipline efforts. If you think about it this way the inner drive for being able to survive will stop your from tackling something which you aren't able to finish. Of course, the irony the reality is that you won't ever finish a project unless you begin it. The process of getting started can be the most difficult part of any task.

The idea of tackling life with the mindset of "All or Nothing" means multiplying the psychological negatives you experience by 10. That means, in reality, you're fighting against your own self. The battle inside will deplete your of the motivation for a determination to achieve whatever goal. A solitary thought can be one of the most important elements in our your subconscious, and is the most significant barrier to self-control.

I have to be perfect

Perfectionists are among the most feared anxiety triggers in life. Its effects include procrastination fear of failure, anxiety, alcoholism and drug abuse, broken relationships and many more. There are times when we experience perfectionism attacks time to time whenever we are scared of making mistakes. However, some individuals are struggling to overcome this false conviction.

"I must prevail in this contest. "

"I must complete this job flawlessly."

"I have to be the very best. "

Note that the underlying aspect of such self-assured perfectionist conversations is the phrase "I should." However, even when the word "I must" is not expressed, the implication/consequence is there. If you believe it is your "must," you will be sucked into an oven of pressure. It is the belief"any failure is unacceptable. "Any inconvenient performance is not acceptable." Human perfection doesn't exist.

There is a certain amount of you realizes that the idea of being perfect can only be a way that will inspire you to search for your best. In fact, this portion of you would like to develop concepts, ideas and objectives and then turn the ideas into real. Yet, another aspect of you, which is that is bound to perfection, does not want to let the ball roll.

You know that the odds are that you will not always be a perfect thing no matter what you try. If you are self-conscious about being perfectionist, the pain as well as the humiliation and self-esteem that comes from revealing imperfections in this archetype can be far too much for them to endure.

What are the consequences? When the part of you who wants to be successful starts to make a move towards the self-discipline door, your perfectionist side is quick to grease the door. This is a way to take away the anxiety caused by your inadequacy.

I Can Do It Without Discomfort

"Maybe I'm just lucky." ..."

"Eat or drink and enjoy yourself, because you'll be happier tomorrow." ..."

"Why put me out of ...?"

They are those who deny the fact that there's no complimentary lunch. If you want to accomplish something unique one must do better to accept that it is necessary to be willing to accept a certain amount of sacrifice or balance. something else.

"Sacrificing" one thing to gain another is viewed as a trade-off between goods offered in exchange for the goods you receive. The "goods" may take a number of form: time, money, emotional and physical health - just for instance. Also, each journey to self-discipline demands that you step outside of your comfort zone.

A person who is unwilling to step outside of their comfort zone where generally, one aspect must be given up in exchange for something else, will never hope to integrate discipline in their lives. Yet, the idea of "Whoever desires something, will cost them the item. Anyone who is celeste will have to pay. "Without penalty, there's no honor" doesn't apply in this case. The reality is that the notion "Whoever would like to have something, will cost his self some thing" can be described as a variant which is similar to "All or nothing" thinking that hinders development of self-control.

In this article, we discuss the anxiety that comes with situations of having to sacrifice some thing in exchange for something else like abstaining from sweet desserts in the course of a weight loss program and choosing to say "No" to many options when there's an assignment to complete or are in a difficult however uncomfortable circumstance that you'd like to stay clear of.

Even if each of these scenarios are painful it's easy to fall into the "all or none" mentality if you keep telling yourself the things you're experiencing are more than being discomforting.

Constantly insisting that things are simple, easy is an excuse to not confront the many fears we have hidden as well as the stress that comes with the aforementioned fears. It is also a method to please the part of us that doesn't want discipline and we do not like waiting or to work.

If we are avoiding an activity Our evasions will generally not stem from the work involved with the actual task. Instead, the reason we avoid it will typically be motivated by an unsubstantiated love that we've subconsciously associated with the achievement of the job. The subconscious thought which triggers this type of defiance is "I will be able to complete it with no any discomfort."

I am unable to change

"Some people can't change. "

"I'm simply lazy."

"This is only a tiny piece of me." am."

"I'm like mom (or dad)."

Have you ever heard such claims? Most likely, quite often. However, no matter how many times you've been told about them, they're just as filled with holes as a mosquito net's entrance. The world is constantly evolving. There is however an issue. There is a classic gag that goes, "How many psychotherapists does need to replace the spotlight or light bulb? One - however, the light bulb needs to be able to accept a change." That's the problem.

There is no way to make anyone other than them want to make a change. the motivation to change has to originate within. If one wants to make a change the person has to first make a conscious decision, and then subconsciously in order to make a alter. The increase in self-control is easily categorized as a shift. It doesn't matter if the discipline will be utilized for the sake of a small or a big task.

There is something about deciding to make changes our behavior, feelings as well as our intellect and all else that we are, in addition to physical issues are the result of the choices we make. A lot of these decisions occur on a daily basis. Additionally, we make a decision every day whether or not to respect the results of certain previous elections Sometimes this decision is conscious and other times it is unconscious. In reality, it's all about the connection that binds our present actions with our previous decisions or experiences.

We're entangled with our past at any time we decide to remain. "I've lived this way for a long time and can't alter." "You aren't able to make an old dog learn new techniques." "I was taught to believe that." ..." that." These statements indicate a lack of the responsibility of someone's life today. Naturally the person we are today and the things we do have a connection to the past.

There will be a terrible incident.

If you open any book on psychology, and you'll discover at the very least a chapter that is about the human's over-inflated instinctive fear of being a victim of a devastating situation. The fear is a mental mechanism created to keep us safe from hurting our own self.

When we confront a situation where we are feeling anxious or uncomfortable, our fear comes from our deepest fears that are expressed in the voice inside us. The voice is an alarm signal: "if you try this then these are potential negative outcomes that may occur to you." So far, so good.

However, frequently, the subconscious mind chooses the most dangerous scenario and then begins to harass you with the possibility of it. In addition, the voice may bring up similar instances where negative outcomes resulted:

"What? Do you plan to speak to your boss regarding an increment? You'll be thought to be complaining and then he'll dismiss you. Do you remember the coach from the team from high school that he dragged you around as an angry complainer in front of the entire team after you inquired if you could change from right center field and first base and you'll never forget the feeling."

"What? Do you plan to deliver an address? The chances are you'll lose the terms, and you'll cause a mess, and look like a fool. Are you able to recall what you were feeling after you did the energy at the front of the students' gathering?"

In the real world it is true that real dangers exist. However, here we are discussing the consequences of self-made, exaggerated dangers that only hinder us, rather than to safeguard us. Keep in mind that the mythology of the movie, Something Very Bad will happen, operates in a subtle way, and hides itself in various ways.

Are you having difficulty in pursuing the goal you've set because you feel anxious each time you make a move towards the goal? If yes, you should look at the things you say to yourself regarding the goal you've set for yourself. You will be able to tell when you believe that the idea "Something terrible will happen" is in place.

Chapter 2: Procrastination In Our Daily Life

O MODELS THAT EXPLAIN THE PROCRASTINATION VARIABLE

The psychodynamic model is according to Baker

Procrastination is described because of fear of failing and concentrates its focus at understanding the motivations behind those who are unsuccessful or quit activities in spite of having the ability, knowledge or the ability to perform at what they do. Furthermore, it explains this fear of failure can be because of the formation of dysfunctional family relationships in which the parental role have facilitated the growth of anger and the reduction of the self-esteem and confidence in a child. It was also the first research model that studied the behaviors associated with the delay of assignments.

Model of motivation

It is believed that motivation for achievement is a recurring trait when a person engages in an array of actions which are designed to bring about satisfaction in whatever situation occurs. Therefore the individual has the option of choosing between two perspectives: the hopes of success, or the fear of failure one refers to the success in motivation and the second is to a desire to prevent situations that one regards as negative. If the fear of failing overpowers the desire for being successful, many people select activities where they believe that success is assured and avoid doing things which they believe are complex and prone to fail.

Skinner's model of behavior

The behavioral perspective of today indicates that a behaviour persists when the behavior is reinforced. The behaviors endure because of their effects. Because of this, individuals delay their work because their actions were a form of feedback. They've been able to win thanks to a variety of factors in the external environment, which has permitted them to carry on with the same type of behavior. People with behavioral issues arrange, plan and take the steps they have put off and do not anticipate the advantages from completing the work.

Wolters' cognitive model

The model suggests that procrastination is a result of dysfunctional processing that is based on maladaptive schemas related to disabilities and fears of social isolation and those who procrastinate generally think about their behavior of deferring; people are affected by obsessive thinking in the event that they're unable to accomplish an action or when the time for completing an assignment is nearing and initially commit to completing the task but then begin to develop negative thoughts about the pace of the task as well as the inability of planning or complete it. As a result, they start to express negative auto-thoughts that relate to the low self-efficacy.

LIFE SITUATIONS INSIDE WHICH We OVERCOMMIT to everyday activities

It is not necessary to postpone tasks that are required for us to be able to work on a daily basis. E.g. making it into the banking establishment, buying groceries at the store, visiting the doctor, taking care of your clothing, cutting hair and so on. The result is a feeling disarray, of not being able to attend enough of everything, and frustration caused by the amount of tasks to be completed.

A personal dedication

We hinder our lives from getting better in certain areas. We don't take part in training and do not train. We are not taking benefit of opportunities for personal development, and we aren't willing to quit the habit of smoking. Likewise and do not address issues with our families and so on. It creates feelings of frustration and insecurity. It also creates feelings of inferiority and a sense of stagnation.

Engagement to other people

We fail to meet our obligations We don't adhere to commitments to work. We fail to meet deadlines, do not attend professional meetings Don't prepare for meetings, squander the time of others, etc. This means that we'll lose respect and trust of those around us.

EXAMPLES OF PROCRASTINATION

In accordance with the degree of difficulty

If a job requires a lot of intellect or physical strength There are many excuses for the delay of their task. This could refer to somebody who is planning to complete an internet-based project. He knows many things about the layout and layout of websites and already bought the domain, and created his website, however by having no knowledge of web-based positioning, holds off creating content that will direct users to your site.

If this is the case it is not possible for the venture to remain in operation until the founder chooses to implement all the steps necessary to ensure the website is visited. It could be as simple as undergoing training on position or enlisting the help of experts in the subject to either advise or assist with the job. As long as you delay any option the project won't advance.

Through long and tedious

It is always suggested to ensure that, when establishing a business or an entrepreneur, it's essential to choose a subject we enjoy greatly. However, regardless of whether you are working in your dream position that you've always dreamed of doing but there is always things you're not particularly excited about such as accounting, routine jobs, writing messages or writing the weekly, annual and monthly reports on the company's performance.

The procrastinator waits until the moment is near reaching the deadline for the task. Although it is boring. But what isn't understood and is unable to comprehend, or ignore the fact that delaying the same type of task could cause them to build up until the point that he has to complete them in very little time and force him to put himself under great pressure and risk of leaks of information that are crucial, thereby damaging the efficiency of the entire task.

If you work from home,

The distractions can be numerous when working at home. it is a huge commitment for everyone. But, it is one of the most difficult obstacles for someone who is a perpetual delay-seeker. It is easy to find the reasons that distractions provide as you begin the day's important tasks for the company or business from home.

Music, TV or household chores desire to relax to take a rest as well as the movement of family members are all reasons those who make a habit of delaying their plans will excuse delivery delays or advancement of their work. In addition, hindering your journey towards success, could cause a loss of enthusiasm for business as the stress it causes could lead to the decision to stop your work.

Fearing the possibility of failure

This is the main reason for people to have given up on the idea to start a business on their own. fear of failing leads them to choose the safest choice. Some people do try and put off the idea, however his procrastinator attitude is evident when confronted with circumstances which trigger the anxiety of failing.

This is why you'll find those who are reluctant to give an address or lecture in fear of the fact that their public will not enjoy their presentation, or they make errors with their speech that can cause to them losing the respect of their audience and to be viewed as a weak presenter. There are also those who put off making an appearance in person to prospective investors, if they fear they'll be rejected. It is among the examples of putting off a presentation that significantly slows the development of any company.

MIND MAP OF THE PROCRASTINATING PERSON

Procrastinators usually live under the influence of a series of thoughts which create a chain and lead to procrastination. Here are four of the most frequent mental triggers that occur in the procrastinator's brain. Then, techniques are discussed to combat the issues.

I must do a lot of tasks... BUT:

I'm an eerily thinking person which is why I'm full of concepts.

"I'm the greatest! Also, I'm capable of doing all this and more.

I'm depressed/unmotivated, so I'm not in the mood to do anything.

I'm not sure or undecided. I'm not sure what to do.

I'm aware of the need to finish my assignments... BUT:

At the moment I'm extremely happy about my new idea. The idea is so intriguing that tomorrow I'll try it out, I swear.

I am only able to reason when I am under stress. So tomorrow I do, I promise.

At the moment, I cannot find the strength. I'd do it the wrong way So tomorrow, I will and I'll make it a swear to myself.

*I find it extremely difficult to come up with a decision. It is not possible for me to make it happen this way, but tomorrow I will be able to, I swear.

We know that you will not and it's crucial to, when faced with these notions, to take into consideration these aspects:

You must place your self under the supervision of someone else to supervise and control your work.

Avoid deadlines. Always evaluate the work.

You can stimulate your mood.

The work environment is overly complex and needs to be reduced.

Avoid doing work on your own and without supervision. Make sure you are able to reduce the amount of work as well as look for methods to reduce the amount of work.

FIGHTING PROCRASTINATION

CAUSES AND COPING STRATEGIES

Cause 1.

Since you aren't happy with the job, this task or the job; therefore, you leave it out until you are able to.

Strategy 1.

Explore the possibilities of automatizing the process, delegating it to others, or transferring it to an associate.

Cause 2.

You don't know how to deal with them.

Strategy 2.

Ask for help.

Get assistance.

Learn.

*Take it.

Cause 3.

Because you lack time.

Strategy 3.

Organise your space and schedule your time. Set aside a certain time each day for achieving your goals. Prioritize:

differentiate what is urgent and important.

Cause 4.

Since you're not sure whether you're going to accomplish what you've set out to accomplish.

Strategy 4.

Examine your objective by analysing your present situation. If this isn't a top priority for you, then turn off the idea and move on.

Cause 5.

You have locked your doors, and want to boost your efforts to start.

Strategy 5.

It's a matter of getting the time to begin your brain. can have a tough time beginning. If the size of your target is overwhelming and makes you feel overwhelmed, divide it into smaller tasks. Split and conquer!

Cause 6.

You need time to think.

Strategy 6.

This is an innovative postponement that's just and appropriate. It is important to take time to think prior to beginning. Once you've done that you'll feel ready and everything will flow easily.

Chapter 3: Mistakes To Avoid At All Costs

One of the primary aspects of learning is to not to make the common errors. Like I say every time that, at times, prior to running faster it's better to take off the stone sack carried in our backs. It will help us improve our speed using similar effort or even less which we are currently using.

If you are prone to delay, here are the three most important things to keep in mind regarding this issue.

Avoiding Structured Procrastination

The term coined by Professor Dan Ariely refers to the increasing trend of performing small tasks which give the impression of progress rather than progressing in the more important tasks that is the one which is left to come further.

An example you put? Create lists of tasks and mark items off. Because it is which is tangible and quantifiable and tangible, we're gaining points, yet everything that is important is unified. Complexity doesn't provide us with the sense of accomplishment in the short term which we long for so and yet they'll be those that provide us with an actual benefit when time comes. A certain time comes around and I'm sure you'll find the time is very swiftly passing. As soon as a year has passed looking back, and we contemplate, "I had put myself to work for what I've always had in mind. Now I'd be able to look back on a year of learning and work to go."

There's no need for this email interruption.

The temptation can be strong when we tell ourselves "I require some time off. If I have just ten minutes to respond to emails or WhatsApp which are piling up then I'll disconnect small amount, then relax and return with a greater force". This isn't the case. The study conducted by the University of London found that continuous messages decrease mental ability by a factor of about 10% IQ points. It's a similar effect as not sleeping at evening.

The Dangerous and Slippery Slope

The reason for this is the belief that if we apply just a bit or even five minutes without distraction, it is not going to change despite the fact that we have seen earlier that it is not able to allow us to relax or gain the strength. What is 5 minutes? It's not much, but what happens is you give into the temptation. Once we start looking to Twitter or Facebook and start to walk on a slippery and dangerous slope. Our attention will be absorbed by the distraction until, before we even realize that, five minutes are now one hour, and even more, it's very hard for us to put down.

Resuming the primary task will be a hill. The brain is in turmoil, we are not in a good mood, and we come up with excuses. We fell down the slope and sank much deeper than the five minutes. The same thing happens with procrastination. Therefore, the most effective way avoid falling into this trap is to avoid to be in the same situation.

The moral of this story isn't to begin smoking marijuana. The key is to comprehend what field of play we're playing on and to apply these easy steps. Avoid them and you'll be safe. Like Oscar Wilde said: "I will resist anything but an urge." It is therefore ideal to avoid exposing yourself to this temptation as we don't need the strength to fight it.

Get it done right now!

It is all about the fact that at all times we do what we would like to do and we're performing what another person wants. This may sound like a lot, but it's true. The constant advertisements grab our attention and the phone vibrates and the thousands of objects push our attention across various directions. No matter who is the developer of the mobile application we're playing with and the user who continues emailing demanding messages or the business behind the TV advertisement Everyone is looking for our time as well as our energy and cash.

Do you believe this is a radical approach to think about the issue? Not at all. What time it takes to accomplish what we need to complete here is extremely constrained. In the real world, as we will discover, it isn't any issue with time however, but of energy and that is also more restricted within the human body as compared to time. If we don't use it for what we would like to build, then we'll make use of it for what other people would like to build.

Let yourself move is an illusion. The belief that the universe has conspired to benefit us is an untruth. The truth is contrary. When we are in flow through the water, we're taken by others to locations that they wouldn't. A benevolent flow doesn't take us to a peaceful beach, where our desires can be fulfilled. It is a constant battle to be swayed from a multitude of directions to take on things other people would like, purchase and invest our time according to the wishes of other. This is becoming increasingly frequently over time, and in an aggressive way.

What is the reason for this? Since we must know the place we're in the middle, and if we don't understand the issue then we won't be able to comprehend the significance of this explanation.

This is crucial since every professional understands that at the core, the challenge is not having a clear idea of what needs to be done instead of putting on their best each day, no matter what is happening, and doing that task that they are aware of is required to complete.

Days pass by, but most important is being worked on. We make a million excuses in our head and spend hours on end with hundreds of tasks yet what's most crucial remains in the pending section. It's not getting any better in the right direction, which creates a huge stress.

To get to the point we want to are going isn't an act of genius it's a matter being able to accomplish what must be completed every single day whether we'd like to or not. And procrastination is a major obstacle between us and our attempts to stop from doing it.

Let's take it to the ground with this:

You can take care of your financial affairs right now.

"Roving up immediately is a good idea since most are inclined to put things off until the future.

Anything you do not take care of right now, you'll be forced to complete someday.

If you don't act and then you'll be stressed thinking you must to get it done and it is also the case that it is impossible to forget about it.

If you are unable to immediately do it place it in your calendar and note in the day as well as the time.

Reorganize your life in a way that you are able to respond quickly.

SELF DISCIPLINE IS THE WAY TO PRODUCTIVITY

WHAT IS SELF-DISCIPLINE?

Discipline means the ability to perform what you have to do at the time you're required to, regardless of whether you are comfortable with it or you don't. Ability to choose a topic and then do it is an ability that is a skill that can be learned or developed.

The mind isn't keen to learn anything regarding self-discipline since it desires to have the freedom to behave according to its own will, simply because it's boring or it's not wanting to perform something that ought to be working, but it doesn't want to be controlled.

Then, when you face all the obstacles you could ever imagine You feel (make you think) it's complicated or difficult but, if you're unable to overcome it and you have to do it, you choose time to delay it. In reality, she doesn't would like to tackle the work and delays it until a later time which is why she is hesitant to do the thing you'd prefer to do and convinces you to not take it on.

When she is in charge quickly, goals set are now a chore that is difficult to accomplish go to the gym, take fewer calories or better nutrition take more time reading, being more loved and attentive and on.

... and this is when your hopes continue to fade away before they are completely gone off your website in the end, leaving you with disappointment that this time or not - you have achieved the goal.

Imagine what you can accomplish when you follow the right path of action with your highest plans, no matter the reason. Imagine telling your body, "You're overweight. You lose 10 to 10 pounds." If you don't have discipline in your life, the desire will not be realized or be realized. However, if you're disciplined enough and discipline, that intention will become an actual truth. Personal discipline at its highest is reaching that point at which, after making a deliberate decision that you're almost certain that you'll move forward with the decision.

The discipline of your personal life is among the numerous tools to personal development available to you. There is no cure-all. The issues self-control can resolve are crucial as well, and although there are many other methods to deal with these issues however, it is the personal discipline that shatters the barriers. The discipline of self-control will help you conquer all addictions, or reduce the extra weight. It will end the cycle of procrastination (procrastination) as well as disorder as well as ignorance. In terms of the issues it is able to resolve, self-discipline is unbeatable. But it can be a very effective element when paired with other methods like determination, passion, and arranging.

This is the reason self-discipline comes to the table many advantages, for example:

The more organized you are, the higher confidence in yourself and your personal pride. The confidence you have in yourself will increase rapidly.

It helps you build power and the ability to tackle the job, take on or tackle whatever task you choose to undertake and succeed in whatever you set out to accomplish.

The more time you spend practicing self-control and self control, the more you'll appreciate yourself and feel good about yourself. The more likely you are to improve your appearance, and will think and see in an more positive ways about your self (a)... and more you'll feel content and confident).

We guarantee your success.

You'll do better quicker and more efficiently.

THE FIVE PILLARS OF SELF-DISCIPLINE

My method of how I create self-discipline can be best explained through the analogy. The personal discipline of a person is an exercise. Training more to strengthen yourself, the better you get. Less you train and the less you train, the weaker you get. Like everyone else, with various muscle strengths and weaknesses, everyone has distinct levels of personal determination.

Everybody has something If you are able to wait for even a moment that's a sign of self-control. However, not all have acquired their discipline in the same way.

The same way, the most effective method for developing self-discipline is to take on challenges you are able to succeed at but may be a little too difficult. It doesn't mean attempting to do something only to fail daily, nor is it about staying in your comfort area.

There is no way to build strength from lifting an amount you cannot move. Nor will you gain the strength to lift weights too heavy for your needs. Start with a set of weights or challenges in your current range, however they you are not far from your top capacity.

Progressive training is when you will increase your challenge after you have succeeded in your challenge. If you are working at the same weight, you will not become stronger. Similarly, if you don't test yourself, you won't develop your discipline.

While analogies such as this can be a bit sloppy however, I've had a fantastic performance out of this. If you push the limits every week, you are staying in the realm of your abilities and get more powerful over time.

When you're doing your weight-training it is important to remember that the effort you put into it is not worth the. There's no benefit from moving a dumbbell and down. The benefit is derived from the growth of muscles. When you improve your fitness routine, you get the benefit of what that you've accomplished along the way that makes your workout superior. It's very satisfying when the training you've done results in something useful and builds your strength.

In this article we'll explore the five principles of personal discipline in greater detail.

Acceptance

The initial one of the five foundations of self-control is acceptance. It is a sign that you see reality with accuracy and can consciously acknowledge what you are seeing.

The concept may sound easy and straightforward, however it's not easy to do in reality. When you are experiencing persistent difficulties within a specific area of your daily life. If that is the case, it could be a high chance that the cause of the problem lies in an inability to accept the reality.

How can acceptance be a key element of self-control? One of the most fundamental mistakes that people make with regard to self-control is the inability to comprehend and acknowledge the current circumstances in a timely manner. Are you aware of the connection between self-discipline and training for weights? If you're able to succeed in exercise, the initial stage is to calculate what weight you are able to carry right now. What is your strength at the moment? There is no formal program of training until you discover what you're doing right now.

If you're not conscious of the current state of your life regarding your current level and discipline level, it's unlikely you'll make any improvements in this area.

I would suggest identifying areas where your expertise is lacking, look at the current situation identify and accept your base point and then create an exercise program that will help you enhance your performance in this field. Begin with a few simple tasks you are confident you will accomplish, before moving to more difficult challenges.

Willpower

Willpower is the capacity to determine a course of action. It is also the ability to say "I will!"

Willpower is a powerful yet temporarily boosted increase in power. Consider it a propellant that is only used once. It's fast to ignite, but when it is handled with care it will provide an explosion that you require to break through inertia and generate a constant acceleration.

Willpower is the ability to concentrate your force. You put all of your energy into and then make an enormous movement. Your strategy is to attack your issues in their weakest areas until they fall apart the ice, allowing you to move further into their territory, and then eliminate them.

Willpower can be applied in the steps below:

Select your desired goal

Plan for attack

Follow the plan.

If you're willing, you'll be able to be patient and take your time following steps 1 and 2. until you are at 3rd step, you must to go fast and forcefully.

Avoid attempting to solve your challenges or problems by using an enormous amount of determination every single day. Willpower can be a drain on your life If you attempt to make use of it for an extended time, "you will burn to ashes." It requires an amount of energy which can only be sustained for a brief period... In most situations, the energy can be consumed in a matter of days.

Work that is hard My definition of work is a an issue to you. Why is this challenge vital? What could be better to handle

A majority of people choose to do what they find easiest and ignore the work that is why you need to be the exact opposite. The opportunities that seem to be the most appealing are viewed by millions of people who are looking for the easiest tasks. the most challenging problems, generally speaking will have more competition, but give you more chances.

If you're able to take on the toughest tasks You have access to an array of possibilities only a few people are aware of. Being able to take on the difficult thing is similar to possessing the lamp of Aladdin.

The benefit of doing hard work can be that is it's universal. The hard work of a person can produce good long-term outcomes, regardless of the specifics.

Work hard and pay dividends. If you can do more perform, the more reward you will reap. The deeper you go and dig, the more treasures you will find.

Healthy living is a tough task. Maintaining a healthy connection is a difficult task as is educating kids. difficult. It is a lot of work to organize. Making plans, setting goals to achieve them, as well as staying ahead of the waves can be a challenge. The same goes for happiness. (true joy that is the result of confidence in oneself, not fake satisfaction from denial and avoidance).

The hard work that you do is a prerequisite for acceptance. Your life will take on an all-new level once you cease avoiding and frightening the work. Be a friend of him instead of his foe. This is a great instrument to be at you.

Dedication

The three lighthouses of Hay three guide you and bring you to the right place determination, discipline and commitment. When you have these qualities three, you can live a life that is bright and optimistic.

Columbus was adamant about discovering the truth about something. He was chosen in his work, and dedicated himself entirely to. Da Vinci was an avid lover of art, he knew and abided by the rules of art, and dedicated his life to creating masterworks.

Every valuable person has been full of desires were realized through perseverance and commitment. Three values motivate the most successful inventors, champions, and exceptional beings in any discipline.

Gandhi, Martin Luther King Martin Luther King, Gandhi and Teresa of Calcutta were also committed to these ideals and left a positive impression. It is certain that you'll achieve your goals when you seek to do something with passion that is organized, and are persistent. It's your responsibility to decide what is the best option approach, then apply it and offer all you can to make your life better and the people you cherish.

People who are content and settled take care of themselves and know how to control their mood. They have devoted themselves to self-control, and are not caught up in the main impulses. Make it your own, because the most effective investment in your life is to stay even-handed and balanced. Control your mind and it, your entire daily life.

An effective tool is taking time to look at your own behavior and discover the source of your issues. you. Following that is finding inner peace, and ensuring no one who is affecting you as you acknowledge it and transform the issue.

They are not either good or bad as long as they're handled by loving. The way we view envy and hate as a negative thing, but they can teach you something If you think about it.

You're wise when you manage your emotions and control your own life and your reality. Through discipline, determination and determination to your goals, you open a new way to reach your goals and resolve the issues of your life. Your life's outcome is a result of the choices you make to do, and you will always harvest your seeds based upon the choices you make.

Persistence

Persistence refers to the capacity to keep doing something, regardless of the emotions.

If you accomplish a great target, your motivation goes through fluctuations and ups. At times, you'll be motivated however, other times, you'll be not. It's not your motivation itself that results in success but the way you act. Persistence lets you keep doing what you are doing even if you're not inspired to take action And the outcomes accumulate. In the end, one of the positive results, desire to succeed is evident.

We should always strive and never stop trying? No, of course it is not. Sometimes, surrender is the most effective option. How do you determine when it is time to quit?

Is your plan still right? If not, then it is time to update the plan. Is your goal still right? If not, you should upgrade or let it go. It's not wise to cling to a dream that doesn't inspire you anymore as well as persistence doesn't mean the same as a lack of determination.

This was a challenging lesson to grasp. I've always believed that it is important to never quit when you have establish a goal and you have set it, stick and keep working until you have achieved the goal. The captain is sunk with the ship, and everything else. When I've completed the project I began and felt extremely guilty for the project. After a period of time I realized this was not true.

A constant and deliberate effort to improve myself is the only thing I want to do. The importance of perseverance doesn't come from holding onto the past It comes from an outlook on the future such that you'd do anything to see the dream come true. Persistence in action is based on the persistence of your vision. If you're certain of what you are looking for and what you want to achieve, you'll be more consistent and resilient when you take action. Coherence in the actions is what will result in the consistency of the outcomes.

Chapter 4: Action-Oriented Self-Talk

While almost everybody knows about self-conversation however, a few are aware of how it operates. In the case of self-talking, a lack of knowledge can be as useful as having no information. Self-conversation is an effective method which can effectively counter Hyde's strategies. In order to make self-conversation work to your advantage, you need to understand its three fundamental prerequisites. It should be positive Specific, Specific and present tense.

Let's examine the entire conversation that occurs in self-conversation. Self-conversation is always on the go even when you don't notice it.

This is true, you receive constant messages from your self which never cease. Each day, you have to make decisions in response to the messages. When you choose whether to eat or the clothes you wear, or take action, a process of choice takes place. Your choices in determining your choices are made dependent on your own your own self-conversation.

In the background, there are arguments and disputes in our minds that we don't listen to, but which profoundly impact our emotions, thoughts as well as our behavior. So you are constantly controlled without your awareness that it is happening.

Are you a fan of to watch TV rather than working on the task that you've been putting off? The reason is that the portion of you that would like to finish your homework didn't get the chance to take part in the debate.

In replacing the negative subconscious thoughts with positive and specific messages, and also in the moment, you'll discover that the power of self-control will be immediately improved. The simple idea will transform the way you live your life. I've witnessed people who have tried this for one week and surprise themselves by their achievements.

When your self-conversation in the conscious mind says, "I should work on my report/task" or "I must be working on my report,"" The message that your subconscious is hearing is "I'm doing nothing with my report or task." This doesn't prompt you to focus on your task or report.

If your mind's subconscious believes you're doing something that's what your hands, feet as well as every other component of your body would like to complete. At the same time, your unconscious brain will be focused on ways to organize your task or report.

The words you choose to use in self-reflection has an enormous effect on how your unconscious mind will work for or against your. If, for instance, you state, "I can't ...," instead of "I decide not to ...," it conveys to your unconscious mind that you are in a position of no choice to make a decision in this circumstance. This creates an incapacity or helplessness regarding your actions and can weaken your judgement. "I pick" ..." means that you can make a choice to make.

Also, if you think "I should ... " or "I must" ...." it," you are telling your brain that you don't have any influence over what you do and that something or someone beyond you is the one in charge which doesn't help you push yourself to achieve your objectives. Therefore, I have always stated, "I choose such a particular thing ...," that, after all, is generally true.

Additionally, you should be cautious when you make sure you use "should ..." This implies that to your mind the decision you make comes out of guilt. This can reduce your self-control.

PRODUCTIVITY AND THE PERFECT BALANCE

HABITS AND LONG-TERM VISION

A vision is an enduring goal. This is the goal I wish to attain for my personal advantage, and the benefit of my family and contributes towards my contribution to the development of my neighborhood, however, it must be something I can achieve with effort and determination. It's goal is to direct your lifestyle as you face changes and to reduce the risk of getting lost. To develop it the process can be guided by these questions:

Who am I?

Where will I be going?

How will I appear to be in the near future?

How would I like to be perceived in the near future?

As we've already seen that the anxiety of not being successful in achieving what we want is among the primary motives for the procrastination. However, this doesn't mean we must give up your dream of becoming more like ourselves however, perhaps we need to shift our mindset.

How do we achieve our objectives and goals with no anxiety caused by anxiety about the future? What is the answer? Habit-building.

Habits are the results of a behavior that we often repeat. In every day life there are many routines we follow including taking off our shoes before leaving the house, turning off the lighting before going out and brushing our teeth in addition to many others.

These are the tasks that we can perform automatically as we've performed the same actions a number of times them in our routine which is why they don't require us to focus or work in order to perform them.

Habits can be described as being deeply established and able to be carried out effortlessly. It is expensive to alter routines. One of the most important factors in forming routines is to ensure that one gets used to routine activities. Thus the activity is built in the routine of daily routine and is performed with no conscious thought.

For you to create a habit it is necessary to:

Absentiment (by the desire or obligation) + the knowledge to achieve it, and the time

If we are considering changing our the way we conduct ourselves or inventing something completely different, it is important to consider the following factors:

A few small steps can be beneficial.

It is vital to keep practicing regularly

It is vital to try out innovative strategies.

We would like to break the task into smaller sections.

We must incorporate this change in our routine right now.

Scheduling is the perfect tool for helping you to keep track of different habits and to maintain consistency.

Rewarding ourselves is a great tool to boost our good behavior. Be careful not to use them with a negative intent.

Chapter 5: Transforming Goals Into Habits

Everyone has either large or small goals are ours to accomplish in a certain time. Many people would like to make millions of euros by the time they reach 30 and others want to shed ten pounds before the start of summer. Many people also would like to publish a book over the next 6 months.

If you decide to pursue some vague or intangible idea (succeeding or wealth and health), happiness, or even success, ,...), typically the first step is to identify the concrete goal. What do you mean by success? What is the amount of money you require? What criteria do you use to determine your overall health? What can you tell whether you're truly satisfied?

However, you must be aware that your goals are not the only thing that matters The most important thing is the way. In the case of personal goals, your path includes your routines.

Habits are the processes that operate on the background, and help you live your best daily life. Effective habits can help you attain your goals while bad practices hinder your progress. However, the habits you have can be powerfully affecting the environment around you.

Your results will not change over time as much as your habits.

The distinction between routines and objectives is in the semantics of them, and they require different ways of actions. Examples:

If you're looking to master an entirely new language, then you are able to choose to be fluent in 12 months(goal) or you can commit to doing half-hour of practice every day(habit).

If you'd like to continue reading You can establish the target of reading 50 books before the end of the year, or choose to take books along with you(habit).

If you'd prefer for more time with your loved ones and your family, plan for ten hours a week together with them(goal)or decide to have dinner in your home each night (habit).

If you're looking to improve the way you live your life, you usually make a list of goals. While many self-help' experts recommend using objectives, the method has several drawbacks.

Goals come with a deadline

Like the beginning of the other side the goal itself is just one moment in the chronology of life. Be aware that the journey continues even following (not) reaching the objective. Many individuals return to their former situation after they have achieved a objective.

Your goals are based on variables they aren't always in your manage

The success or failure of the goals you set is dependent on many aspects, all of which are yours to are in control of. Injuries can hinder you from reaching your fitness objectives, or you fail to reach your financial goals due to the fact that you've needed to repair an expensive piece of equipment. A family illness can affect your mood and can hinder your creativity targets...

The goal setting process can lead you to be feel smug or even reckless. Scientific research has shown that the brain is unable to distinguish between the process of visualizing the results you want to achieve in the event of planning to achieve the desired result. This is particularly true when you share with others in the surrounding environment about your objectives. Additionally, goals that are unrealistic could lead to risky or illegal behaviour.

In contrast to goals, that require continuous effort and constant effort, habits function on autopilot. The goal is to build an array of carefully selected routines that gradually lead the steps towards achieving your goals. This method of planning has numerous benefits.

Once established, the habits will be in effect in a way that is automatic.

It could mean we go beyond our expectations

and the habits are simple to master.

"Adopting habits is for life..

The habits of our lives can influence other areas that are not obvious.

TO CONCLUDE, THE SEVEN GOLDEN HABITS.

It has been proven that most of us lose three hours of our time each day as a result from bad practices. The consequences of these habits are a lot on our work schedule and impact the quality of our lives.

How do we fight these issues? The cultivation of seven positive practices will allow us to manage our time and control our lives. It is easy to incorporate them however, implementing them requires the discipline of a professional. But once they have become habitual, it will pay off over time.

Decide on where you would like to go. This is related to the idea we talked about earlier. Goals can be a way to accomplish this but visualizing your ideal lifestyle is even more effective because we wish it to be continuous and never ending.

Decide on what you'll need to accomplish to reach your goal Be aware that you'll get what you plant. If you're required to alter your life, make them by stepping back. You can't possibly do it all in one go, which makes you have to pick.

The first thing that is most crucial 20 percent of of our actions generates the majority of our outcomes. Find that 20% and pay attention to the 20. Beware of the urge to focus on the first thing that isn't small, easy and familiar. Consider what's most important before it gets urgent.

Make sure you assign only the proper time and then delegate the appropriate people: Plan every task according to the correct time and only then. If you give yourself a small amount and you fail when you delegate you too much you will be aiming for perfection in the group but not for each job. Set aside time rather than projects. Be sure to ask yourself what are able to delegate and how.

You must follow your plan: Create a schedule of your activities that you will complete every single week. Next steps are how you can move your project and goals towards success. Your day should begin according to your plan unless something crucial happens. Do not get caught up in the tendency of being distracted by delays, issues or unexpected issues that are not considered to be a top priority.

Concentrate on a specific problem and complete it: The culture we live in overvalues efforts and taking action. A busy person is deemed to be that they are important and so the action can become unavoidable. The mind can only handle one thing at time. time which leads to anxiety. Moving from one problem to the next increases the time every one consumes. This doesn't take into account the work you do, but how long you work on it.

It's easier to live your life It's your time is yours. It is essential for all the things you'd like to do or do that you enjoy. Do not waste your time. Make sure you take care of your body. It's the most basic instrument. Keep your spirits in check as it is your vitality as well as your power. Find a balance between your passions and your responsibility. When you are organized, you'll have plenty of time for the things that interest you. It will be easier to accomplish more in much less effort.

Chapter 6: Make A Plan Take Action Now And Get Things Done

Plan your actions and begin to turn that plan into a realisation. There are things that we would like to achieve and goals that we want to accomplish and trips that we'd like to undertake. But there is something that stands in the way of us from achieving our goals, which is a refusal to act now, aka the TAN.

I've never met an individual who did not have a goal. Sure, we may not all have the same goal however, everyone does have a wish. The world is split into those who act right now to achieve their dreams as opposed to those who do not act now and fail to realize their dream. If you're one who isn't taking actions and doesn't move toward a goal or a goal, or and a plan and a goal, you don't have any reason to be unhappy about the actions and results that are the result of those who act now.

Take a look at this instance. Fans of basketball typically talk about the poor score on foul shots by Shaquille O'Neal. I believe that just half of his shots were successful. It is not a problem with the percentage because the guy TANNED. He acted now and was a part of the NBA and was thus able 50 percent successful in the foul shots he took. The fact is, I didn't take any action to play in the NBA thus the total number of foul shots I've shot during NBA games are zero. So, I don't have any right to complain or speak negative about O'Neal's free-throw rate.

The story of the foul shot highlights the fact that those who act now even though they're not successful in their efforts, are more worthy of than people who take the initiative today. Take action today since sitting around in a corner is not going to get you done all the tasks that are required. If you were planning on going back to school in the past couple of years. Have the preparation and sitting around your desk affair been going for you?

If you're in your couch, planning but aren't taking action it is likely that you'll still thinking about going back to school within two years. If you're serious about returning to school instead of just contemplating returning to school now, you need to take Action Now. Get up, obtain an application form for college and study the criteria to apply. Now, you can begin taking action to fulfill the criteria for acceptance.

It's not easy. It will surely take for a long time. It will take time regardless of whether you're doing something now, or just thinking about and planning to act in the near future. What's different is that if you act right now, you'll get closer to achieving your objectives. It is imperative to take action today as you will be the person who steers your life's journey. As you relax and let whatever comes up take place, you're the seat of a passenger in your existence. Just like when driving passengers have very small impact on the route that is traveled.

If you do not take actions now, you're in a slumber and ought to be standing and moving. If you sit and let the world happen instead of taking action is like the person who takes the knife into a battle. Your preparation is sloppy and uninformed. You should take time now to think about the things you're going do and the way you'll act now in order to accomplish it.

Make today your day to make an action plan, and then follow through with do it now and manage your lifestyle.

Chapter 7: Get Action Right Now Using Mind Maps

It's awe-inspiring to sketch out a strategy and then act now to make your dream a reality. Mind maps are the process of organizing your thoughts and ideas in a graphic method. Mind maps typically is based on a central point or thought at the center, and the entire thing spreads out. Mind maps use circles and lines to display connections, relationships and necessary steps to be followed. One of the most appealing features that mind map diagrams offer is how they can tell the whole picture in one glance.

Mind maps used to be made using a pen and paper. Nowadays, there is a large amount of mind mapping applications that are available. If this is a new concept to you, don't purchase an expensive application. Test a trial version for free or two to find out which fits most closely with how you think and how you operate. When you've mastered the art of it, you'll be able to purchase an expensive program that comes that comes with lots of bells and bells. I've been using computers for mind mapping software for over five years. I chose a program that can sync to my tablet, laptop as well as my smart phone. I love being able to make a list of things on the computer, and then carry it around to my tablet, or even use it with my smartphone.

There is no difference if you're using an old-fashioned pencil and paper, as well as one of today's latest digital programs, you can start the process of creating a mental map to arrange the tasks that need for you to act now. When you've got your thoughts sketched out either on paper or right in front of your eyes begin by following your plan and begin taking action right now. The way you organize your mind map will allow you to go beyond planning and move on onto the actual work. Be aware that the primary goal of creating a mindmap isn't to create an attractive image. It's about getting the thoughts that you have in your head and into the open so that you are able to clearly understand what you must do and how each one of them is related to other tasks.

The first step to start right now is implementing your strategy. It is not logical to start a new project without a clear understanding of what you're planning to accomplish. Mind maps are an application that permits users to visualize their choices and quickly draw connections between concepts. Mind maps allow you to connect concepts in innovative and intriguing ways that often can lead to fascinating problem-solving outcomes. Mind maps allow you to create plans you can communicate easily to others and keep track of your progress. Mind maps allow you to monitor what you've completed and the things that need to be accomplished quickly at a glance.

Mind maps are tools and ways of giving directions. Be aware of this while creating the mind maps. There's no way to do it. Mind mapping is an instrument, so make use of it to aid you in doing the job. The mind map should be created in the way that you think and be sure that it is flowing according to the way you think. The connections I draw between two thoughts could differ from the connections that you draw. The differences in these are what makes personal mind maps valuable tools in deciding whether to act today.

Imagine something you'd like to achieve and then create an outline of your mind to illustrate the steps you need to take to accomplish it. Take action right now to complete it. It will be rewarding to experience the sense of accomplishment that deciding to act now based on your mental map can bring.

Chapter 8: Use Vision Boards

It's fantastic to make use of vision boards to assist you in your efforts to move forward. Many people have goals they would like to achieve and goals they want to achieve and travel plans they'd like to take. But there is one obstacle that stands in the way of their progress, and that is a refusal TAN to take action right now.

Vision boarding can be a powerful device to assist you in deciding how to start taking action today. In the past, vision boards were real physical boards that are covered in photographs, images, and words. The vision board was designed to display both the goal you want to achieve and the path you'll take to reach it.

Nowadays, vision boards may be also electronic. There are a myriad of resources available online, to acquire photographs or to create images one's own create electronic vision boards very easy to create. If you don't have your own photos for vision boards, look out websites such as Photopin as well as Pinterest. It is possible to use sites like Picmonkey as well as Canva for adding words and extra effects to your images.

If you create your visual board you gather images of what you want to see in your real-world scenario is, and then you make the collage that represents your reality. My goal is to stay in good form. The vision board I created had images of grass, sneakers and an amazing dress I'd like to wear due to my efforts in getting into good shape.

In order to make your vision board an important tool you can use to get started right now, present images of your goals as well as photos of the way you will get to your intended finish line. For my getting more fit example, I'd need pictures of healthy food choices and fitness routines.

It is crucial to display the way and the why on your vision board, so you can ensure that every time you glance at the board, you'll be aware that you will not arrive at your dream destination through accident or luck. The idea is that you can reach the destination you want to go with the help of perseverance and a lot of effort. Visual representations of your tasks as well as the goal will allow you to make a decision now to complete the task. As you examine the picture and notice the ways to accomplish it, you'll have an incentive to complete the work and act right now. The work transforms the vision board beyond a vision board into an image of the work you've accomplished.

There are a few concepts which help to explain how this process is effective. The concepts are the law of attraction and radiation as well as the law of desire and intention. It is a simple concept that is that whatever goes around is re-circulated and reaps the seeds you plant. Also when you're looking for to get something, you must put in the effort required to obtain it. For the older computer users GIGO garbage in garbage out. For a more specific method, vision board works by taking action today and complete the tasks required for your dream to be a the reality.

It is essential to keep some things at hand when it comes to vision board. First, you need to remember that vision boarding isn't an appropriate time to stick a lot of beautiful images on a poster board. This isn't the time to add a plethora of adorable photos or phrases on the Pinterest board. For the best results and efficient, you should create an individual vision board to reflect every goal, area or aspect in your daily life. Make sure you put your own photo on your vision board. This will provide you with an ever-present reminder that your visual board is about yourself and your goals it is not an exercise in abstract thought.

Be sure to talk regarding your board and images as if they happen right now, at the moment. This is the concept of bringing things into being. In addition, when you talk about the vision boards, you should use only affirmations, positive thoughts and phrases.

A vision board can be an amazing tool that can give you a clear vision of your objectives so that you are able to take action today and accomplish your goals. Get your materials together, make an image board and utilize to get started today.

Chapter 9: It Is Fun To Act At The Right Time And Place

Make a decision now, because it's fun to act now at the appropriate time and location. Through the course of any plan it comes to a point that one needs to move from planning and talking to taking action and executing. One of the most interesting aspects about getting started is that if you decide to act at the correct time it is an enjoyable act to perform. Making the appropriate decision at the right time results in lesser stress, less irritation and better outcomes.

The concept of the existence of a time and place, or time for everything that exists has existed for as long as humans have lived on earth. Ancient texts like the Bible reference the notion that all things have the season. There is the time and place that is suitable for every thing that exists. This passage speaks of the idea of a time to plant and the time to reap and the idea of a time to be joyful and the time to grieve. Also it is the case that there is an appropriate time and a place for all things.

The reason why this concept that everything has the characteristics of having a time and place has endured is because it's factual. A lot of actions are best when they happen at a specific time that is the proper time. For baking cakes, as an example then the time for putting all ingredients into the oven comes when they've been put together, not earlier. Making the decision to place the cake batter into the oven can result in failure if it is done initially, but will result in success when completed at a later time. If you are assigned assignments to your work, you must complete them by the time to finish them prior to the due date, not later than the deadline has been passed.

Another method of putting it is to pose the question, "When did Noah build the Ark?" The answer of course, is prior to the flood. Noah did his thing in the correct time and at the appropriate location. If Noah had built his Ark after rain began falling, it could be already too to late. Noah didn't stop at making plans, or taking measurements. He took action to take action right away and constructed the ark at the appropriate time and in the right place. It's crucial to act now, in the appropriate time and in the right place.

It is the basis of the field of science known as inertia. The concept behind it is that a object that is at rest, tends to stay in a state of rest, while an object moving tends to remain in motion, unless it's influenced by an outside force. Also, when you remain still and wait for events to occur, it's simple waiting, sitting for a while, and then sit and wait. However the moment you get moving taking action right now in order to complete your tasks It is much simpler to continue moving in the future, and to keep taking actions now to complete the task.

The path to success is when you act now, because you are doing what must be accomplished to get there. Take action today you place the cake into the oven after it's been made. If you act now you construct the ark prior to the flood. By taking action today to prepare yourself for war during time of peace. time when peace is restored. That is, if you act today, you dress like a grown-up and perform the things you need to do to be successful and complete your tasks.

If you're wondering if you'll have the time to get started to get things accomplished It's easy. It's the time is right now. Make a decision today to complete your tasks since they won't get completed unless you do something that is of a certain kind. It is the people who are successful that are taking action today to accomplish their goals. Perhaps, those who act now to accomplish their goals will achieve the conditions for success. Perhaps success comes as a result from taking the initiative now to accomplish your goals. Whichever one of these theories is true or relevant at any time in time It can't be denied that all begins with the decision to make a decision right now. Make the decision today, in the appropriate time and location, and reap all the advantages of achievement, satisfaction and success in getting the job accomplished.

Get started now, because it's enjoyable to act at the appropriate time and location, and that will help you get your work completed.

Chapter 10: Now And Control Your Life

Make a decision now and take charge of the destiny of your life. One of the most effective examples is presented in the next story.

Five birds were perched on a wire that was a telephone when three birds decided to travel to Florida to spend the weekend.

Questions: How many birds are left?

Answer: Five. Because making a decision to act isn't the same as doing something.

This tale is a great method to illustrate the distinction between taking action right now and making plans. Planning is essential, as it's the initial stage in completing tasks. However, planning on your own is not enough to get things accomplished. To get the job done, it is imperative to start immediately. Instead of deliberating to plan, arranging and even plotting and plotting, three birds leapt into the air and flew off it would change the course at the end of that wire. If the three birds that were so busy making decisions, were to take action right immediately, there'd only be two left along that wire.

It's crucial to get from making a decision and then executing the action. Planning, thinking and planning are crucial tasks to complete. The significance of these three tasks is not to be undervalued and shouldn't be undervalued. In the at the same time it is important to remember that making plans, thinking about and plotting do not suffice. After these are all accomplished and the action must start.

It's as simple as taking a trip with your family. If you don't take action the family members and your spouse are going to plan your vacation, and you'll end up at that particular spot you've always wanted to avoid ever again. However when you get involved today and begin the planning of your trip You are in charge. The vacation planning process will be influenced by the activities, location as well as accommodations. If you act today and begin the planning for your trip it will make you more likely to be able to take pleasure in your getaway, and relax enjoy the company of the people you travel with.

In the same way, when it comes to work when you sit back to find out what the opinions of your customers or employees are it is a way to be a shopper within your company's life. In your company it is your responsibility to take the lead. If it's time for your work day to begin every day, it is imperative to start today. Every morning, you must begin implementing things that are in your business strategy. Do the necessary work to help your business grow. When you run your company, if you act right now, you can control the future of your company. This is crucial because, the majority of businesses are founded in order to feel in control and make those crucial choices that make the ultimate decision for an company.

Also, it is important to be aware that you only have 24 hours per day. However, no matter who one is, there are only the time of their lives for 24 hours. If a person begins having a full-time job and at home, she is able to take action today, everything is done and she's in charge of her business and life. Although it's nice to travel on a train but it's much enjoyable to play the role of conductor, to steer your train along the tracks you've laid out and have the responsibility of blowing the train's whistle.

Whatever we do, the world moves ahead. Life isn't in a state of stagnation. It happens, and even when we don't do anything whatsoever, the world continues to change. This can be a challenge that is a problem for people who don't act now. The reason is that if you don't immediately take action and you are not in control of the manner in which the pieces are moving on the board. If you don't start taking action then you're stuck sitting in a position of passive. It is like sitting around watching others determine what you should take action and when you'll perform it. In contrast If you act today, you're in your car for the rest of your life. If you act now the things will happen as you choose and in the way you'd like them to happen. It is much more sensible to you decide on the way your personal life is in the matter.

Chapter 11: Now Look At Time And Place

Make a decision now, while understanding that the opportunity comes with the time and a place. If you act now then you can seize the opportunity and, to make it easy take action as you're supposed to do. It is crucial to act now, in the event that action is necessary. There's time and a time and place for everything, and if the action isn't performed at the correct time it will result in an expense to be incurred.

In the field of economics, there's an idea of opportunity costs. The chance cost represents the cost of making a decision that is not made in situations in which one has to make an option because there are many options that are not available all at once time. This is why it's crucial to act immediately. If you don't immediately take action at the time you need to be doing so, you'll miss out on this chance.

Imagine it as connecting two airplanes. How would you feel if the way towards New Orleans, Louisiana from Philadelphia, Pennsylvania? Imagine that there's an accident in the route to the airport. You have to wait in the rush hour traffic for two hours. What happens if you go for lunch at an eatery and you get delayed for by an hour or two. If you are delayed in either one of these situations it is likely that you'll miss the chance to catch the flight that connects Philadelphia towards Atlanta. If you don't make it on time to Philadelphia to Atlanta and you miss your flight, you won't have the chance to take the flight connecting Atlanta until New Orleans. If this happens, you will have to go from the airport or take a meal out can is a cost to reach your destination on time method.

The timing of your visit is vital. In the real estate industry it is the rule of thumb

"Location and location." In all aspects of life, the mantra should be "timing Timing, timing, time." Timing is crucial. The timing is what makes what makes the difference between success and failing. For a successful event, being in time means arriving minimum 15 minutes earlier. Arriving at the start time is to arrive in the wrong time. Being late is not acceptable. The timing is crucial.

It is important to learn how to be proactive now since everything depends on you making the right decisions at the proper time. It is the time to terminate an employee occurs when you discover that she has been taking advantage of others, not after they have been doing it for six months. If you permit employees working for you even once you have discovered she's the victim of theft, it will cost you the chance to recruit to train, retain and keep a trustworthy employee.

The time to be ready for war is the time for peace. What you accomplish, now has a significant role. There is no action until it is initiated. If you delay until start of the war to plan for battle, it will cost you the chance to collect items, gather soldiers and prepare an effective strategy for fighting. If you do not immediately take action when it will be required, there's the chance cost to be payable.

Don't be scared to act today. Be confident about the consequences that your decision to act now resulted in. Instead, you should get started now and accomplish the things that need to be completed. Opportunities cost very real. Sometimes, it is visible as lost money. In other instances, it shows in the form of stress and tension. Another way that opportunity costs show out is through the choices you are no longer able to make. right to make. The opportunity comes with costs that is real and the best method to reap the maximum benefit out of your chance costs is to start taking action in time to take action.

Make a decision now, while understanding that opportunities have an time and a place. Act now, so your chances for success and happiness don't pass your way.

Chapter 12: Suck It Up And Move Stop Refusing

Get it out of your system and make a move until you put aside your hesitation to act right now. There is no doubt that in order to be successful at all endeavors, you must reach an point at a time that one needs to leap into action despite the apprehension of the fear. It's a great idea to make goals, formulate plans, and imagine the grand visions. They are all activities are all part of our lives during various time. We must however, go between dreaming and planning, to performing. In order to achieve our objectives it is imperative to act today.

There's always a reason that justifies the inaction. There's always a deadline that's impossible to meet or obligations to family members as well as financial burdens such. In order to be successful, you have to discover a way to get rid of your way out and get moving immediately. My daughter and I were both hit by a hit-and-run driver that we later found out was a frequent drinker driving. The day was among the worst that I have ever had. After we got hit and the car was speeding off as I lay on the street, looking for my kids. At that time all I wanted was to sit and cry, however I couldn't. I was forced to make the fucked in and move. It was time to get moving right now to get the job done.

This was real-life that was not a show on television or blog post but actual reality. The only way to get it right was to act right now. I was required to stand up to find my children and arrange for medical treatment and contact my husband for a visit to the hospital, make arrangements for my children's siblings and it went on and on. The moment was the time to let it all out and hold on to the anxiety of the future, tears and anxiety for a different time. The time was time to get involved now.

Let's look at some typical excuses and discover practical ways of overcoming these excuses.

Impossible Deadlines

If that is why you're not taking steps now, it's time to get rid of it. If deadlines are ones that you've made, it is time to take a seat and take a real-time assessment of how long it would take for you to complete your tasks. Then, you can create deadlines that are based on your own life circumstances. If they aren't those you have set, or are beyond your control, then you should rip in and acknowledge that your plans may have to be revised or won't be able to be completed and plan alternatives to take.

Family Obligations

If family obligations keep you from pursuing your goals today, you must look at your schedule first. You should take time to take the time to review your schedule for family and personal and in depth to determine the best way to arrange your schedule to give you time to complete whatever needs to get accomplished. This could involve making the effort to work with your plan before your family members each day or staying up late after the kids have gone to sleep. Consider your timetable in a realistic manner and make decisions according to your obligations instead of the ideal lifestyle you'll have someday.

Financial Burdens

In the event that you aren't able to get cash for your plan keeps you from getting started right now, take a look at your budget and decide the things you could do with, and what you could do differently or the ways in which you could "rob Peter to pay Paul." These financial obligations are just the same as other reason to take steps today. The majority of people believe that financial resources are, to avoid be precise, finite. It means that the vast majority do not have an unlimited amount of money. If your finances prevent your from doing something take steps to modify your strategies to fit the financial obligations you face or figure out a method to improve your financial situation by restructuring your obligations and selling your assets, or obtaining another work.

If you've been sitting in the shadows of your own life, scared to act now because of deadlines that are impossible and family obligations, or financial obligations, quit making excuses. Instead, begin moving forward toward your dreams, plans and objectives instead of straying getting away from your goals. Eliminate the excuses in your thoughts. Remove the barriers. If you're struggling resolve the issue. Take it down and make a move to take actions now.

Chapter 13: Get A New Attitude For Real

Make a move now and adopt a new mindset and reach your goals. A few people have the goal but never achieve the goal. Other people dream about the impossible and achieve it with style and grace. There is certainly some differences between the two women. There is a difference in their lives that could be an extremely tiny one. A woman who has the ability to achieve her goals just needs to take action today.

We've all seen those who say they wish be successful, achieve lofty goals, and to feel content both professionally and personally. We know those who achieve and reach their objectives. However, we also have people who don't meet their targets and are convinced that they'll never get there. There is a difference in both cases. is only a small one. It's a matter of doing something now and adopting the proper mindset. The people who succeed in one area or the other are often approached by people who come to them for assistance, guidance and advice.

A few people that seek advice, they hear it in one ear, and out of the other, never taking the root. It's like seeds thrown onto a rocky surface that's neglected and not watered. People search, seek the assistance, advice, and advice and create an enormous, gorgeous and amazing. They take the guidance take it, and use it to improve their lives, and later go out to give their gift to those around them. They are like seeds that are planted in fertile soil which is watered and tend by a caring hand.

Successful people taking action today and have a different mindset that those who do not succeed when they try. They take action right now and start taking action now, also known as TAN. This means they begin to move and work toward whatever they would like to attain. People who are successful have a positive mental attitude, believing that even the sky doesn't have the limit to their goals. They follow the SMART (Specific measurability, attainable realistic and time bound) strategies. Success is simple. The key to success is a simple one Get a well-defined strategy, act now to implement the plan and become who you would like to become.

If you're a person who has not a practice of operating under the mindset of take action today Be encouraged and believe that you are able to succeed. it is possible to be the person you would like to become. Make these easy steps:

1. Don't work without a plan Instead, remember that if you don't prepare, you'll be unsuccessful.

2. Start now to start creating your strategy, and get moving forward in your goal

3. Make a change in our mindset and begin believing in yourself as a an entrepreneur

If you want to achieve success, think of yourself the seeds could develop into a stunning field of blooms. Be sure to take care of yourself, give yourself a break and act like the kind of success you desire is right across the way you're taking. The path to success isn't just the goal of a select few It is a goal that anyone has the ability to attain.

If you act now, you will be able to gain a outlook and realize your goals.

Chapter 14: You Have The Ability

Make a decision now and realize you are able to accomplish this. It requires some time and effort in order to develop the right plan of action that can enable you to take the necessary action to achieve a goal that you've set you or complete a task. If you're gifted and the ability to create an idea, then you've got the ability and talent to follow through with the plan until it is completed.

Jesse Jackson once said, "If my brain can imagine it, and my heart is able to accept it and I believe in it, then I will accomplish it." The statement is applicable to all aspects of the Take Action Now journey. It all begins with a thought. Once you've come up with the idea and develop a strategy, that's where things get started. You must then discover a method to convince yourself in your mind that you'll succeed in executing what you have imagined. Find the confidence to believe you is possible to achieve what you envision. It is essential as once you've convinced yourself that the possibility is possible then you'll be able to act today and start doing the thing.

A lot of people have amazing plans or brilliant goals they wish to achieve. A few of them do not arrive at the point that they act now to finish the plan, or realize their dream. The most common reason for this is they feel they don't possess the capability. The majority of the times the truth is that this isn't true. If you are able to create an SMART strategy, it is possible to carry the plan. An SMART plan that includes:

Specific: A goal that is specific is one that clearly defined start end, goal and finish that must be achieved

The markers can be measured in the strategy in order to assess if the objective was achieved

To be attained - also known as smart, the target should be one that is able to be accomplished by the planner.

Realistic - The objective must be realistic in the way one looks at the individual and all of the components in the equation

Time-bound - A smart goal should include an time to be completed as SMART goals cannot last forever.

If you've created an SMART strategy, also known as one that is precise and measurable, achievable as well as realistic time dependent, you've created a strategy that will be successful. Now is the time to continue but it's not the time to find reasons to not act immediately. Keep the fact that there are several common errors which make people believe they can't take action immediately to implement the plans they have in mind and be successful. Although these are serious however, they are solvable.

1. Skills-based - If not possess the necessary skills you'll need to start today, don't despair and you are able to acquire the knowledge you require. You can find online classes or university classes, and professionals in your field who will give you advice and suggestions. If you realize that you don't have the necessary skills to carry out the plan you created, take a look at your plan and modify it. You can add a line to your plan that requires that you acquire the expertise you'll need, and then start taking action right immediately.

2. Money - If you do not have the funds needed for you to begin taking action on your plan, review the plan over again, and create an entirely new section that lays out the amount of money required and

the best way to get it. Are you in need of the help of a loan from your bank? Are you looking to convince your friends to invest in your? Do you require another job in order to achieve this? If you think that financing is the only thing hindering you from taking action right now, you should amend your strategy with ideas for the financing you need and get moving to secure the funding needed.

3. Courage - If the insecurity causes you to think that you can't do anything now, then it is possible to change your mind. It's one of those instances where you need to dress in your best pants and get moving. Also, in other words there is a chance that you are scared to take action. You might be worried that things could go incorrectly, but continue to move regardless. Be honest with yourself about your fears simply push yourself forward.

If any of these issues are preventing you from taking the step to move forward right now, make the necessary measures to eliminate the shortcomings and take the necessary steps immediately. Remember that making the necessary steps to address these issues is an opportunity towards action right today. As you're striving to fix these shortcomings Be encouraged by the fact that you're doing something right now. Utilize that energy to keep working until you are successful at achieving your goals.

Chapter 15: Getting Out Of The Loop

What is the most compelling reason you give? Every person has a reason they hang on to that they believe they can justify the current situation. Perhaps you're overwhelmed and do not have enough time and you need to get up in the early morning hours and arrive late into the evening. You must look after your children as well as cook and clean. They're real-world situations that are not fabricated. is it a fiction. However, using it as a reason to not have established your own company is an untruth. Whatever your schedule may be, it is important to be able to take a minimum of 30 minutes to yourself. The majority of us watch "Real Housewives of Some Shocking City" during your free time. You can spend anywhere between two and three hours watching other women who live their best (fake) life.

Now, let's talk about it for a second. There's nothing wrong with you and you've just not had the time to pursue your goals. It's not that you're broke, it's just that you don't put your cash on the things you want. The problem is that you're allowing fear to keep your behind. Although you may not be actively fearful, but this shows by your thoughts, behavior and in your lack of progress towards your objectives. According to a blogger on leadership as well as the editor of platforms such as Business Insider and CNBC, Benjamin Snyder, fear causes the person to avoid situations which could alter your life. The fear of losing your feelings and goals, as well as allowing you to make many excuses.

When you are aware of your fears and how they affect you, you are able to rephrase the fears or imagine them as new and empowering methods that will help you achieve your goals, rather than slipping away from your goals. In his blog post on CNBC, Snyder (2017) provides a list of obstacles that prevent us in achieving our goals such as:

The fear of failing. Everyone hates failing. There is no reason to undertake things that require your full attention and effort into something only to fail at everything. In reality, failing is a one of the steps towards reaching your objectives. The most important thing is to recognize that failing in something does not mean you're a failing in any sense. Therefore, if you set out to create your own beauty company and does not succeed, it isn't an indication of you simply because you don't have the necessary techniques for making your business successful. It's good to know that the skills you need to master can be developed in time. This means that you'll be able to attempt to improve your skills in the future. However, once you've acquired the required capabilities, you're sure to achieve success.

The anxiety of being insufficient. But the truth is that there's no need to have all the knowledge to take on an endeavor. Being afraid that you're not good enough or unqualified to begin a new business is not uncommon. But, what it does will hinder your progress. One of the biggest issues with feeling unworthy is that a lot of people aren't willing to improve what they think they're incapable of. Being aware of your shortcomings will not propel you to move forward. Instead, it's better to believe that you're embarking on a journey of learning and that's why you'll be prone to making mistakes as well as fail at least once as well as face challenges that which you've never encountered previously.

Fear of uncertainity. It is impossible to know for certainty where your journey is going to lead you. The uncertainty of life makes many people uneasy. This is not surprising, but if you're not sure of how to prepare it is possible to get in trouble. Actually, wandering around in the dark is not a pleasant experience. Entrepreneurship is a risk, but the danger doesn't seem too overwhelming; you either fail (and get experience), or earn millions. Yes, a lot of things could occur during the course of your business however that's part of the appeal of the game and it's essential to understand the fact that it's a game.

Fear of a tragedy. One of the problems with a lot of people is that they're used to thinking about the worst-case scenario. There's a fear that you'll fail the big time, and that you'll be losing a lot. We tend to overstate the stress and suffering we'll find ourselves suffering if we do fail to accomplish some thing. However, when you lose it, you'll always be able to get your self up. But what when you don't think about what the worst that could occur? What if you could fill your thoughts with positive outcomes that could happen instead?

The fear of change. Being hesitant about changes (good or not) does not make anyone feel at ease. We're comfortable with our existing comfort at a level where thinking about any shift (even even if it's positive, such as sipping champagne aboard a private plane) does not feel right. It's possible that you believe that you're not worth the alteration. Many people think that money is unclean and worry that they'll be assessed if they earn massive amounts of income. A few people worry about the volume of task they'll need to perform and aren't certain whether they'll be able to handle. However, how do you tell when you've never tried?

The fear of judgement. Humans are social creatures. Most of the time we have been able to create great connections and relationships in our relationships with one another. However, it can also lead to judgement as well as ostracism from a group in the event of doing something that isn't considered normal. However, this fear of judgement can also be driven by our own fears and fears that others will consider us "weird" (like being an TikTok celebrity or selling bright leggings to make a profit) and yet nobody has said any of it. If someone does judge on you, the reality is that it has nothing to do with you and has more related to their own insecurities and self-limiting ideas. The onus is your responsibility to dispel your critics' opinions.

The fear of being rejected. The fact is that not everybody is going to like your idea or what you provide. This shouldn't deter you from getting your name out in the market because people who could have liked your idea may also be left out. It's inevitable to be rejected in the business world and you need to develop the ability to stand up for yourself and avoid taking it personally. Nobody is denying you for who you are; they're simply saying that the product they use isn't specifically designed for them. All it is is personal preference (preferences you've developed too). All you have to do is go to the world and discover your tribe. It may take as many as maybe 100 or even 1000 to get that"yes!"

FEAR AND COGNITIVE-EMOTIVE LOOPS

It is possible that you have observed how one fear can lead to another one or links with the other ones on a scale. This is the problem with anxiety and fears as well as negative or fearful thought patterns; they just perpetuate many of the same ideas that can result in what's referred to as cognitive loops. Jim Dethmer (2018), co-founder of the Conscious Leadership Group, defines cognitive-emotive loops as follows:

The repeated pattern of ideas and convictions create emotions that help us feel right about the stories we tell ourselves, which will then intensify our thoughts in the next step. They consume energy and stand behind development. It's one of the ways that we human beings get stuck. (para. 1)

The thoughts and emotions you have are putting you in a constant circle of unproductiveness. It's difficult to contemplate it. What's worse is knowing that a lot of people can't get out of these loops.

Let's take the anxiety of feeling inadequate to illustrate. One of the most prevalent thoughts is: "I'm so stupid." This can create a feeling of being unmotivated in your self-esteem, demotivated, and lacking confidence in yourself. Then, you look for concrete evidence that reinforces these feelings. If you make a post regarding your business plan via social media but there is no response, or anyone asks you questions about your company that you aren't able to immediately provide an answer to, it strengthens your thoughts and feelings. Instead of locating the solution or finding a new platform that can promote your company, you decide to give the effort because you are afraid of not getting the same result emotions, thoughts and even feelings.

How to Get Out of a Cognitive-Emotive Loop

There's a good thing: it is possible to escape from these mind loops through an effort that is concerted. It is important to consider the bad habit as one that has developed over time as well as poor habits may require a few weeks or even months before you can break them. This means that you have be patient with yourself. Three strategies can assist you in getting from your mind's loop. Try all three before settling on the method that works for you. You can also combine all three until you reach the state of being free from the endless cycle of negative thoughts and fears. Be aware that whatever works for you might not be effective for someone else.

The Inquiry Method

This allows you to research the reasons behind the reason you're feeling and thinking the way you are. If you see an idea that comes into your mind which says that you're not enough, or the thought that people are going to laugh at your appearance, make note of the thought. You shouldn't be scolding yourself to think about the thought. Do not be angry at yourself for constantly worrying about your self-esteem and worrying about what others think of you. It's just important to acknowledge that you're experiencing the thought and observe if there are physical changes in response to that thinking. Are you experiencing a faster heartbeat or are you feeling like sinking in your chair? Maybe you feel dehydrated, stressed or fatigued. Inhale deeply out, and begin your inquiry.

Think about what you did before that moment and what the reason was. You might have tried creating your own Shopify store but was stuck in a rut feeling like a complete idiot since Shopify is supposed to be a simple platform, but you're still struggling. It could be that nothing really happened while you were contemplating your idea for a business you thought about people enjoying it came into your brain.

Ask yourself if the idea is true. Is it really a blunder or do you think Shopify somewhat difficult to grasp when you're just developing it? Are you able to prove that people laugh? Has that occurred before? It's almost certain the result of being hard on yourself and there's nothing or no proof to show that your thoughts are true.

Then, think about ways to think differently and identify ways to take action directly related to them rather than abandoning like you would normally do. Consider telling yourself that you're not stupid It's just a matter of making a decision at first time. This is like walking for the first time. You're likely to fall. Your next step is to look up YouTube and ask the Facebook group made up of Shopify or e-commerce shoppers whether they've had the same issue previously and what they did to overcome the issue. If you are afraid of judgment it is possible to get at minimum two others to tell you about their thoughts on your idea, and receive real-world opinions, not only what's within your mind.

The Journaling Method

As with the method above journals allow you to note your feelings, thoughts, and events as they happen. It is usually the most effective method for those that aren't sure of how they feel. The act of writing things down may provide more clarity more than simply contemplating the issues. When you're feeling down take note of it. Write down as clearly as you are able to describe how you're feeling. Note down the event that brought you to begin feeling this way. This could have been an idea on its own or perhaps an experience which triggered the thought.

Within a week or two take a look at your journal and try to discern any specific trends. You might be constantly thinking or feeling in similar to yourself walking to work. Perhaps those thoughts show out when you're with specific negative people. If you're doing something specific, the thoughts pop up and you need to figure out ways to escape them. If you don't see any patterns in the meantime, you can try again for an additional two weeks. Review the journal entries over again, and look for patterns.

There are ways to handling them according to the way that they manifest. In the case of someone who causes you to feel depressed and self-conscious, it's possible to break the ties to that person (you shouldn't require external negatives within your own life). If you're unable to simply move rid of them, you should tell the person what their words and actions affect you. Discuss with them the goals you're aiming for and what you'd prefer them to do to be supportive of you. Many people are willing to listen, and they might not realize they're making you feel down. If your thoughts pop in a specific time for instance, such as on the morning commute to work Find ways to make the drive more positive. It is possible to listen to a podcast that focuses on the subject of entrepreneurship, or even your personal development.

Stop-the-Negative Method

There are times when you have a clear idea of the thoughts, feelings or even the reasons behind these feelings, but you are unable to clear them from your mind. It's not that they're blocking you from doing anything however they force you to slow down as you may not wish to go through excessive growth in a short amount of time. This way it is possible to choose a feeling that you would like to become the North Star of feelings. You tell yourself that you wish to be full and feel a sense about abundance. Perhaps you'd like to be able to think creatively and have positive thoughts.

If a negative idea comes into your head, should not entertain it. Say no thanks and remember that your goal is to be able to create abundant and creative thoughts and nothing other than that. It is important to capture your thoughts within the initial 10 seconds they appear within your head. Recognize them, but don't become angry over the thoughts or attempt to ask the reason they're in being there. What's the point? They're not meant to be in the place. Replace them with positive and continue forward.

FOR THE WORKBOOK

Whatever technique you pick you should find that you feel empowered and educated. It will take some time for fears and negative thoughts to go away. However, they may not go away entirely, but they won't be able to hold this grip on you any longer. The workbook I've included not taken note of an Inquiry Method. It is possible to write your thoughts on a paper alternatively, or end your negative thoughts to replace them with positive thoughts. Consider any of these options during the coming week, and observe how you think and how you feel.

2

50 SIDE HUSTLE IDEAS

"I

Don't have an amazing business concept." Another of those excuses that we often use to stifle us. It doesn't require an incredible business plan to launch an enterprise. Actually, the majority of incredible companies began as simple concepts. Netflix began by selling DVDs; Amazon used to sell books, and Facebook was simply a web site that allowed college students to talk with each other. The possibilities are endless to turn any concept that you're working on into something incredible once you've mastered the capabilities and the infrastructure. A few people make excuses that they're trying to save up enough cash to start, or locate investors. From my experiences it's exactly the people who use their money on food and clothing, and don't have a plan for their business to give. What if your business idea is already inside your head? You'll have to convince anyone to offer them one million dollars of their hard-earned cash to help you think of something.

If you're not sure of an idea for a business yet or are uncertain about whether your current plan thought of will be successful or not, take your time and don't be stressed. We'll outline 50side businesses that you can get started within a few minutes or weeks with only a few resources. It's not necessary to be able to put aside thousands of dollars or find an investor. It is possible to leverage the skills you already possess or attend an online classes to understand things you're not aware of. It is necessary to spend some time. The only aspect you aren't able to control when you start a company. However, even if you get 10 minutes throughout the day, lots can be accomplished in the tiniest of moments. The fifty side hustles I'll be sharing will be organized into five main segments.

SELLING PHYSICAL PRODUCTS

Physical items will never be out of style. The people love the appearance and feel of physical products, and if are able to build a strong company around the products you sell, you'll have the chance of having a successful enterprise within the next few years. It is possible to sell tangible products via your own store online, like through WooCommerce or Shopify as well as offer them through marketplaces such as Amazon and eBay. It is also becoming more popular of selling goods via social media platforms as well as fintech and software businesses are expanding in this field to make selling on social media even more simple. When you have a clear idea of what you're looking to sell You can then go the way you'll offer the item.

1. Made-to-order beauty products for women The market is growing for soaps made by hand and personal care products

that are made of essential oils and seeds. Many people are working to promote chemicals-free cosmetics and those that have pure ingredients and have evident benefits. The ingredients can be sourced as well as packaging locally. Based on the budget you have set, you'll need to begin with a single product, and develop other products as the sales for your business increase. As an example, you could begin selling a homemade facial bar, which has been proven to treat dark spots. You'll need a few ingredients as well as the required equipment. Create only at least two scents which you are certain your clients will enjoy. Be known as a business which can improve the appearance of the appearance of your face. When you're a good size that you're able to make facial products and masks to sell to your clients and increase your business as you go.

2. Drop-ship clothing: If you are an avid observer of the latest fashions and trends it is possible to create a drop-shipping service. By using drop-shipping, your company doesn't need to store any inventory. Make an agreement with businesses you'd like to collaborate with, and then promote their goods through your website. If someone purchases from you, you'll acquire the items from the business that you've collaborated with. You'll then have them ship the items with no address or names (so customers don't have any idea where the items come from). If you're a drop-shipper, then you'll typically have to charge your own price for items, as the firms won't offer the buyer a price reduction. If you come across the maxi dress you want at the price of $18, you are able to offer it at $20 or even $25. Your price must be based on sense financially (cover your costs for marketing) and be affordable (is the material

sufficient to warrant a price significantly higher than the retail price?).

3. Drop-ship appliances: It's an excellent selection of appliances that can be shipped drop-shipping. The larger appliances can be difficult to store and then ship. Also, they're not easy to market as people do not need an entirely new refrigerator every day. Businesses that offer these items will definitely want to discuss a drop-shipping agreement with you because they'll market their product at '"free." Since they're big appliances, it's possible to increase the markup.

4. Niche baby care products These are items which only a few clients will purchase due to their personal circumstances. However, you are sure they'll keep coming to your shop to purchase additional items. I'll be sharing many business concepts for you to consider on this subject. One of them is

baby items and clothing that are suitable for infants who have sensitive skin. There are babies who have issues with their skin or experience phases of the sensation of having sensitive skin (like the time they eat food that is solid). Many moms will do anything to make sure their baby's comfort and avoid further injury or minimize the risk of the rash appearing at all. It is therefore possible to sell a selection of baby items made of fabric as well as other components that are safe for babies' skin, and free of substances that may be harmful to a baby.

5. Products that are niche, toys and equipment to help children who have learning difficulties education is an essential aspect of the child's development. It's even important if your child has an identified learning impairment. There are many sources to create tools and toys designed for children

who are special, helping to improve their learning speed so that they don't get lost by kids in the same age range.

6. Specialized products, such as exercise equipment and activewear suitable for mothers who are expecting In keeping with the overall theme it is possible to provide expecting mothers with clothing as well as equipment that they would like to make use of during pregnancies. The moms-to-be can be very demanding due to the raging hormones. However, they desire to appear and feel beautiful. This is a needs.

7. Specialized products - drinks and food items that are designed for those who follow a particular diet like paleo, vegan keto, and paleo diets have gained recognition over the last few years. They can make people healthier and more fit by catering to certain nutritional guidelines. It isn't necessary to take on everything.

Select one, search for the best suppliers and market to your customers. Let me mention that niche items are more challenging to find and produce however, they can also yield higher profit. If you are able to find companies who are willing to drop-ship within those niches, it could be more advantageous than buying items at a large quantity.

8. A grocery store online is like the typical grocery store where you'll have a selection of CPGs, also known as consumer packaged products (CPGs) such as drinks, food along with cosmetics, cleaning and other items. However, the delivery time will be less than 30 minutes, and may you'll have a limit on the quantity of products customers can buy at any given time. To ensure that this is economical, you'll need to establish contracts with your drivers and suppliers, along with the firm which is slated to rent you the

warehouse. As you're selling CPGs, it is likely to realize the benefits of their investments within the first month due to the fact that these items need to be shipped swiftly. For those who are wondering Yes, certain businesses are founded upon trust, not on cash. There is no need for funds to begin a new business and you only need the best opportunities. It is enough to have the ability to set up an online store, and then market your company effectively.

9. Print-on-demand T-shirts are one of the easiest business ventures to establish. Are you aware of those adorable T-shirts featuring hilarious slogans? Are there any suggestions for humorous or adorable quotes which could be printed on plain white T-shirts? It is time to start a printing-on-demand business that sells T-shirts. Take a photo of a T-shirt that is simple on Google that matches the style that your

vendor is likely to offer. Utilizing an application such as Photoshop or Canva write your message on the shirt as they could look if printed. Put it up on your site and then promote it on the social networks, your friends and your family. If someone purchases and you purchase the shirt. You can also have the message printed on it. The process won't be terribly lucrative until you are able to purchase many shirts at once as well as own a printer however we have to begin with a place. Printing can be done on various other items of clothing like the hoodies, caps, or even socks.

10. Cups printed on demand for coffee: Coffee enthusiasts are among the funniest people around and will always purchase mugs that reflect their appreciation for coffee, or the personality of their. Start a print-on-demand purchase of cup coffee

(and other kitchenware such as cutting boards, saucers and oven gloves).

11. Marketplace: Do you think you could rival Amazon? Inspire small-scale business owners to post their items for free in your marketplace. They will be able to market their product, and you'll pay a tiny percentage of each profitable sale that they sell on your site. One of the biggest mistakes individuals make when considering an online marketplace is that they have to charge hefty fees for the sole purpose of placing their products in the marketplace. Small businesses are unlikely to want to do this. They pay these charges on platforms like Amazon that have existed for many years, and have the ability to ensure the success of sales. Do not be greedy, consider the long term.

Selling digital products Internet makes it possible to offer anything and including physical items. There is a rising demand for and supply of digital goods. What exactly is a "digital" product? One of the most basic definitions is "a digital product or service that is enabled by software that provides a certain amount of benefit to an person" (Napierkowski 2020 para. 4). What I enjoy with this definition is its usage of "utility." When you find that your potential customer can't use your product in their everyday life, it might be time revisit the design board. There numerous applications and software that help you create and launch digital items much more simple. Furthermore, as there's nothing physical and there are no logistics costs it is possible to create an amazing product at a low price and market it with huge profits.

12. eBooks for nonfiction (autobiography)
The following are two major subcategories for the nonfiction genre: autobiographies and self-help. If your experience was a bit

chaotic and you've done amazing events (this is subjective naturally) it's possible to include your experience into an ebook. We hope that it will help other those in similar circumstances to recognize that they'ren't isolated. You'll be able to see an escape route from the dilemma they're within, should it be it's possible. It's not always a bad idea accept the situation as they are. If you're using the Amazon Kindle Direct Publishing platform, it's possible to get your book printed in only less than five minutes. Be sure to read about their guidelines to ensure your book's in proper format, and that your cover images are of the correct dimensions.

13. Self-help self-help book It is a favorite book for those looking to make their lives better especially in regards to three main categories that include entrepreneurship, wealth generation and financial independence; the importance of

nutrition, health as well as holistic health relationship, locating relationships, and love. Here's an undiscovered truth that you don't need to be an expert when it comes to the subject you select to write about. All you need is enthusiasm and a solid understanding. There are many other self-help subjects that you could write about, such as professional development and home management or even design; therefore you don't have to be a solitary writer.

14. Fiction ebook Are you a writer with an imaginative mind and an imaginary character who is able to go on all kinds of adventure? Why not create an ebook of your fiction thoughts? It is a well-known genre with more people reading in this genre, particularly romance novels for females. You can also do anything from sci-fi to fantasy, and even criminal. We all love a good, mystery that is unsolved.

15. Courses that are fully accessible online

Courses online allow students access to information easily and at much cheaper prices than when they enroll in a college or university. The market for online courses continues to grow, as students, when they have earned their degrees or certificates opt to further their education. It is possible to create an online course in almost any subject. But, I'd recommend going to something that you are passionate about or possess a lot of expertise in. When you've created your course online and hosting the course on your website or through an online platform that offers multiple online classes (like Skillshare, LinkedIn, or Udemy) and has an extensive audience of people who are eager to learn. It's likely that you'll need to conduct some more advertising in the first alternative to attract people to attend your course. But it's an excellent method to create your own network and encourage students to check out what you can provide (perhaps you provide additional products and services). When you offer online courses with full access the students will only need to pay a single fee they'll have access for life to your course online.

16. Online courses that are subscription-based Also, you have the option of allowing your students to pay a per-month fee to access the course content. It is best to do this when you host the content on your own site (most community-based platforms do not allow the option to allow this or even choose how they charge their students). This is also more effective in the event that you've got lots of material and possibly additional services you want to provide (as as part of your cost of subscription). Additionally, when you use this approach it's necessary to constantly refresh your content, including classes that

are already in place, to make sure the content is relevant.

17. Online courses that build-up It is a method that you could use when you need to instruct things that are difficult to grasp through different phases. In essence, you'll guide learners through the process step-by-step of how to do things. Every class should have an assignment for students to complete prior to moving into the next one.

18. Apps for free: Mobile apps permit users to access quickly your services or information you can offer because everyone already has their mobile phones. One of the main requirements for mobile applications is that they must provide an actual benefit. When you use a freemium program that allows users to have access for free to a portion of your content, and then allow access to a premium version at a cost. If you're a fitness trainer and you

have access to some workout videos for free, and also let customers pay for more advanced classes.

19. Premium-only application: If you've got a high-quality piece of material (again it is subjective). If that's the situation, you may make a premium app in which users pay a cost (either either a monthly or annual cost) for access to the app and advantages that come as a member to the community.

20. App for users who are free: You can make an app accessible to users for free. They are able to access all information on the app no cost and must endure ads from brands they may be interested in (relevance remains important here). The app will earn money from these brands through advertisements within the app but and not from the users.

21. Stock photography: If your an amateur photographer or videographer you are able to hold photo shoots featuring models, or capture images of stunning sites and artwork and then sell electronically. Platforms such as Shutterstock let you receive the amount you pay each time the content you upload downloads. Content creators constantly search for quality images and videos to go with their books social media and other materials for marketing.

Chapter 16: Selling A Service

The process of selling a product is basically selling skills you have and people need but don't have the time to perform their own. When you sell digital goods such as this it is your job to show other people the steps to take and then they execute it. However, even with consulting and coaching however, clients are required to perform part of the job. Clients purchase services because they do not have the capabilities to perform the task or aren't willing to commit the time. The price you'll charge for your services could be dependent on your own perception (that is, determined by the value you place on yourself) in relation to how long you've worked to perfect your skill or your customers and the amount they're prepared and willing to spend.

22. Professional writers There are a variety of kinds of writers, however they all need

to have the ability to utilize words to convince or create a belief in the reader can be true or assist them with understanding complicated ideas. Many people who have a background at writing take on various writing positions such as ghostwriting to blogging and content production on social media platforms, as well as screenwriting for blockbuster film. There's no need to determine the people you'll market your writing services once you get started. Find the most writing opportunities you can, and then work towards advancing.

23. Web designer: Designing and building beautiful web pages has never been more simple You don't have to know how to code websites now. Yet, many do not have the time to develop their own websites, and might be unable to figure out the process. This is a good thing for you as

almost all businesses require a website that is active.

24. Graphic Designer: Logo design printed material, printing materials and social media content as well as other graphics for promotional materials are things the majority of companies outsourcing. Also, the advancement of technology and tools make becoming graphic design professionals easy, even if you haven't studied to become one. In the case of example, if you're able to make use of the program Canva and you're in the process of declaring yourself as a professional designer. Graphic designers that completed their studies for this position utilize Adobe Creative Cloud software. It can be a bit complicated to comprehend (and expensive for certain) however it's not difficult if you've got the determination to leverage only one application at the time. When you have

clients, the money earned generated by them can be used to finance the cost of your software.

25. Bookkeeper: Every company requires the service but many are not willing to spend the money. Bookkeepers' task is to keep track of certain financial information that a company needs. Anyone who has basic math as well as accounting knowledge and who can utilize Microsoft Excel can position themselves as bookkeepers. Bookkeepers are responsible for recording financial information However, they don't have to analyze the data or offer recommendations to business owners just like accountants do.

26. Virtual assistants: When business managers of expanding companies become extremely busy, they'll be seeking out someone to aid them with their administrative tasks responses to phone calls and emails, guarantee the absence of

overlapping meetings, publish on social networks, and prepare presentations if required. Based on the individual who you work for and the nature of the business they run, your requirements for requirements will vary. What will be the same the same is that your job will be to make their life (personal and professional) more organised. If you are a virtual assistant you will be able to work with more clients at the same time (and eventually, outsource certain tasks) If you are an individual assistant You can only be a single person's assistant However, you could charge a higher rate.

27. Personal shopper: A different task which can be time-consuming for busy and wealthy people is the shopping. For groceries, clothes and other items for the home A personal shopper could prove to be an invaluable resource. Although our world is now digital, there are still people

who aren't able to find the time and the energy to browse through the countless items. It is recommended that you choose a particular area of interest for you to shop on your own. As an example, working mothers must balance the demands of home and work with baby. Another area to target is fitness and health. Executives who do not have the time to shop for healthy foods clothes, equipment, or even clothing. It is possible to incorporate these in your understanding of fitness and health.

28. Photographer/Videographer: If you already have a passion for photography and videography, you can start to monetize this skill. There are many who say they would like to be videographers or photographers, however they're waiting to save up enough funds to purchase a good camera. I think it's just a lot of talk, and a reason to justify not doing anything. If you

don't own an camera at the moment your chances of being a sought-after photographer or videographer when you acquire a camera isn't going to be happening. If you're in that situation look for a different side hustle. For this to function as an alternative to your job it must be an already-existing skill or passion in which you're using your existing assets.

29. Designers of fashion: not everybody would like to wear mainstream clothes; they'd like to be unique while walking along the sidewalk and say that everyone is asking which store they purchased the item from. Fashion designers, you're able to design clothes to order, which means the client visits you with a list of what they'd like to wear, and what kind of occasion they'll be attending. Additionally, you can design items that you feel people would like and locate the ideal person to wear it on.

30. Makeup artist: Everyone would like to look flawless in her makeup. However, in the real world there aren't many who can do it. If you're looking to become an artist in makeup it is possible to take a few months of education, but you might also be experienced making your own makeup. You may then decide that you would like to pass on your expertise to the masses.

31. Hairdresser: This talent is likely to never be out of fashion. The art of grooming hair for both women and males has been a part of the everyday life of everyone as we do not have the time or energy to spend time the hair we have. Additionally, with the changing trends that come and go, having an expert in hairdressing to stay on top of these trends is crucial.

32. Nail technician: In line with the latest fashions in beauty Nail technicians have been gaining popularity over the last few

years. What isn't changing maybe could be the width of nails that customers want. It's a very popular market. It is possible that you want to master anything nail-related. However, it is also important to specialize in a specific technique so that you can be the person to go to for we'll say acrylic manicures.

33. Event planners: The anxiety and anxiety that accompany the planning of an event can be difficult to deal with. Being an event planner you can help clients think about their day instead of what it will require to make it feasible. This is a different service in which selecting a particular niche is useful. You could become an event planner for birthday celebrations, weddings Or perhaps you'll opt for an alternative to the traditional retirement parties.

LEVERAGING YOUR NETWORK

A lot of people may have seen the phrase: Your network represents what makes you worth it. The adage is basically pointing towards the idea that the more influential individuals you have in your network are, the greater profit you earn. You might have someone offer you an opportunity or connect you with those who require a certain product or service. You are paid to make the connections. Being able to build relationships, meet others or build an audience isn't something that everyone has the ability to do. It's definitely a specific sort of person as well as certain skills. The most extrovert people are the best when it comes to using their networks to gain. It is important not to look at it as forming an online network in order to make them sell something or your data to the most expensive price. Instead, see it as an opportunity to assist people in finding the items and services, buyers or providers they're looking for by utilizing your network.

34. Super-connectors: This is the best business idea for those who are outgoing and easily connects with other people. You're a pro at talking to others and identify the best people to complete any project. The skills you use to negotiate need to be of the highest standard. Super-connectors' job is to link buyers with suppliers. It is possible to make an arrangement with the seller and receive a portion of the money customers pay. Certain super-connectors also have agreements with buyers in regards to purchasing products that are extremely sought-after and challenging to find. There is no need for a platform to begin this type of enterprise, but it's advantageous to use platforms like LinkedIn or other groups where entrepreneurs participate. It is recommended to work with the purchase

of products that cost a lot to ensure that the amount that you get from your deal is worthwhile. Being a super-connector requires lots of time and effort. Not everyone is able to do it So make sure you're putting in the time and energy.

35. The influencer influencer receives a fee from brands (often within the fashion or beauty, food and beverages sectors) to promote their product to their followers on social media. Many consumers trust these influencers due to the fact that they think that an influencer would not support a product which isn't great. People may even want to become like the person who is influential and will go out of their ways to purchase the items they like and use (even even if they're a sponsor). To get noticed (and receive a payment from big companies like Nike and Starbucks) You'll need expand your reach up to hundreds of thousands perhaps millions. In the role of

an influencer, you could be paid a single amount (with no products) to serve as the brand's ambassador for a period of months or even years. You will also be able to continuously advertise the company (wear their clothing or consume food items and shoot photos as well as videos). Additionally, you can earn for a portion of sales over the time you're an ambassador. Others influencers are paid to only take a couple of images and/or videos of the product.

36. Podcasting - hosting interviews: Hosting podcasts is like being an influencer. Instead of making videos or shooting images, you're creating audio-based content. Podcasts typically only begin making profits after growing their audience or following to an impressive quantity of downloads. This is how sponsors know how your podcast's performance. The most well-known

format for podcasts involves interviewing experts from the field of interest (like the business) or with respect to a particular area (like optimizing the brain). When you're launching your podcast, if it's not the case that you meet a large number of well-known or successful individuals it's possible to start by inviting anyone to interview you. When you're more proficient with conducting interviews and the more time you put into growing your fan base, you'll start to see those who want to interview you or even sponsor your podcast.

37. Podcasting is a way to give business or life tips: You don't need to talk to anyone in order to create an audio podcast. If you're an expert with advice regarding the subject or industry you're interested in then you are able to sit front of the microphone yourself and give that tips. Make sure the information or topic that

you provide is relevant and relevant to the intended viewers. Since this type of format isn't so engaging and captivating as podcasts that are interview-style You'll need be prepared to invest a bit more effort.

38. Similar to the way people purchase audiobooks as they are a fascinating (and easy) option to consume the content of books. Many people enjoy listening to captivating romance, crime and horror stories, including the stories of children, via podcasts. Each chapter you write in your novel can become an episode of a podcast. It is possible to create stories is an extremely special talent, however it can be developed with time If it is something you are interested in but isn't your cup of tea, do it.

39. Selling software for affiliate marketing is similar to the super-connector, in that it doesn't require the use of a platform.

However, using a platform such as blogs or a social media could be beneficial. In the role of an affiliate, you advertise a digital item on behalf of the company with the promise of a portion of the sale (usually between 10 or 15 percent). Numerous software companies run affiliate programs of all kinds and use affiliates to boost sales.

40. Affiliate marketing to sell products: A lot of companies that are new to the market in the market for consumer packaged goods (soft beverages, processed food such as health shakes, toiletries etc.) make use of affiliate marketing to increase the sales of their products and to increase awareness about brands. It could make sense as a goal for these items since different brands could have greater market portion. For one thing, the public has had confidence in these brands for a long time.

www.ingramcontent.com/pod-product-compliance
Lightning Source LLC
Chambersburg PA
CBHW071447080526
44587CB00014B/2024